THE WAY OF CHRISTIAN LIVING

John H. Timmerman

William B. Eerdmans Publishing Company
Grand Rapids, Michigan

Copyright © 1987 by Wm. B. Eerdmans Publishing Co.
255 Jefferson Ave. S.E., Grand Rapids, Mich. 49503
All rights reserved
Printed in the United States of America

Library of Congress Cataloging-in-Publication Data

Timmerman, John H.
  The way of Christian living.

  1. Christian life — Biblical teaching.
2. Fruit of the Spirit — Biblical teaching.
3. Bible. N.T. — Criticism, interpretation, etc.   I. Title.
BS2545.C48T55   1987   248.4   87-12455

ISBN 0-8028-0305-9

CONTENTS

PREFACE

The way of Christian living is not a lonely way. One discovers this by looking back, by marking mileposts where others have lent aid and direction. It is good to do that looking back, for it affirms one's own way. Here I have gone, thus have I walked, these have guided me: that is the recollection of the Christian way.

While it is impossible to acknowledge all those who have lent direction to me, let me give special thanks to John and Kathy Van Til. And then to Jeffrey, Betsy, Tamara, and Joel, my four children, to whom this book is dedicated,

> Henceforth I learn that to obey is best,
> And love with fear the only God, to walk
> As in his presence, ever to observe
> His providence, and on him sole depend,
> Merciful over all his works, with good
> Still overcoming evil, and by small
> Accomplishing great things, by things deemed weak
> Subverting worldly strong, and worldly wise
> By simply meek; that suffering for truth's sake
> Is fortitude to highest victory,
> And to the faithful death the gate of life;
> Taught this by his example whom I now
> Acknowledge my Redeemer ever blest.
> Milton, *Paradise Lost,* Book XII

INTRODUCTION

Too often we describe the way of Christian living in negative terms. If we can avoid certain things, and simply not do other things, then we believe we are walking in the Christ-like way. Certainly there are things the Christian should not do; the Ten Commandments, for example, have in no way diminished in authority or reasonableness. Yet, if we focus only upon the negative way, we miss the tremendous vigor of Christian living—the sense of walking in the joy of our risen Lord. The marvel of this positive way of joy is that, properly understood, it can undergird even the times of sorrow in our lives.

Scripture provides that positive way in the fruit of the spirit, a counterpart or balance to the things we should avoid or not do. My intention in this study is to examine those fruits of the spirit as they are revealed biblically, but also to see how they apply practically to the everyday way of Christian living. These biblical fruits are not some strange, mystical goals beyond human reach; they can be appropriated into everyday life and provide the dynamics for Christian living.

That challenge becomes less difficult once we see the dramatic *reality* and *presence* of love, joy, peace, patience, kindness, goodness, faithfulness, gentleness, and self-control. We have spoken of them too often as distant goals toward which we strive. Instead, they are practical *means* by which we live. The wonder indeed is that we find them confronting us directly in the most common routines of human living.

My method in this study is, first of all, to understand these fruits of the spirit in their biblical context. This is the necessary first step, for it grants authority and divine direction for any application we make. They do indeed root in biblical teaching.

Second, we want to understand the relevance of these biblical fruits in everyday life, attended as it is by sorrow and joy. Rooted biblically, these fruits flourish in human lives.

Since the nurturing of spiritual fruit may be seen not as a dramatic, momentary spurt of growth but as a steadfast way of living, we also distinguish between two ways of living: the way of the world and the way of God. Proverbs 11:30 states that "The fruit of the righteous is a tree of life, but lawlessness takes away lives." Finally, then, in order to walk in the way of Jesus, and to develop the fruits that root in the tree of life, study questions and reflections appear at the close of each chapter to guide personal or group Bible study.

CHAPTER ONE

Packaged Lives

My neighbor had a voice as gravelly as a streambed. He had farmed a quarter section of rocky Appalachian soil for over fifty years. When I passed by, wheeling my son in the stroller along the dusty road, he would jerk his old body over to the fence that held his few cattle and pigs back from the road and would chat in a voice that sounded like stones rubbing on each other.

The crooked three-strand barbwire fence didn't always do its assigned task. I found his prize sow in my garden one morning, delighting itself in the fatness of fresh lettuce. My neighbor came walking slowly down the road with a small sack of grain and led the sow back by dropping portions behind him.

When he leaned on the fence to chat, he tipped his sweat-stained hat back so that his forehead looked like a tall, shiny pillar between the sunburned nose and the hat. He let his body slouch loose like a half-full sack of feed against the fence, a man used to working hard and knowledgeable in taking his ease when he found it.

The subject when we talked was always the same: these modern times don't hold a candle to the good old days. "Why, these times . . . ," and on he would go about the evils of our age. I saw the times through different eyes, but much of what he said was true. True enough to make me question of myself, then and in the years since, what one thing could be said to typify our age?

In an age such as ours, where change seems to thunder in huge storms and nothing holds still, how can we begin to specify one thing? Is it the relentless change in moral values—the devaluation of life and the elevation of desires? Other ages seemed to be more secure, more stable. Perhaps change itself is the thing that typifies our age.

As with all large questions, large answers provide only part of the truth. If we say that values change, we have to ask why. If we say change itself typifies our time, we have to ask how.

If we find such answers too large or too vague or too puzzling, consider this: the one thing that typifies our age as no other, that makes it and us unique, is packaging. A surprising response, perhaps, but only because packaging has so infiltrated every aspect of our lives that we are hardly aware of it.

Consider just one example of packaging from consumer life, a vitamin pill. The chemicals are first mixed and packaged in a capsule, which in turn is packaged with ninety-nine other capsules in a plastic bottle, which in turn is sealed and packaged in a carton of a dozen bottles. A dozen such cartons are placed in a large, heavier cardboard box, and such boxes are packaged inside trucks or railroad cars for shipping.

The elaborate process of packaging goes from chemicals to carton to your grocery shelf, where the vitamins are also packaged in a display area of the shelf. Why all the bother? For one thing, it is easier to package many small items into large groups. Our age is one of mass transitions, of volumes. Small things don't count as much as large things, unless the small things are diamonds that one can package in a vault. And packaging protects the product. At each stage the packaging grows thicker and harder. Finally, packaging makes products more appealing. Anyone who remembers taking a spoon of cod liver oil in those "good old days" can appreciate that. Who wants to take chemicals by the spoon when you can take them in a brightly colored capsule? Who wants a plain brown bottle when you can buy a box of vitamins decorated with flowers or cartoon characters?

How many of these packagings appeal to human vanity! And how many of our dollars go over the counter for that reason alone. The packaging by advertising—of everything from cars to political candidates, from carpeting to homes—has developed into a psychological warfare in which the primary weapon is human desire, the goal is the winning of many dollars, and the victory march leads to the bank.

The art of packaging is the art of making things appear better than they are. If the advertiser can come up with a snappier package, a more clever commercial, then people will buy that product. But inside the package we still find the child's toy that, despite "five simple steps of construction," won't go together. We still find the cereal that, despite its promises for a slimmer, trimmer, happier you, tastes like recycled coffee grounds.

We labor under a mistake, gripped by a mystique that seduces us from reality and from a Christian way of living. Television advertising during the annual Super Bowl broadcast costs over one million dollars per minute. How can a producer package the product, dive through rational thinking to the strange world of subconscious desires, and convince the viewer—in one minute—to purchase the product? The packaging is everything. Make the customer feel delight; make the customer feel desire; make the customer reach for it.

Does it sound familiar? We have heard it before—in Genesis 3:1-7. The serpent was the most subtle creature alive. He gave Adam and Eve a most remarkable package: "The tree was good for food . . . a delight to the eyes . . . and to be desired." The seduction of the subconscious by clever packaging is a story as old as Eden, and our wandering east of Eden has ever been in pursuit of the same thing: satisfaction of our own desires.

Let me give you an example of twentieth-century packaging that will unnerve you—as it did me. As it did sixty million people to be precise.

Imagine a string of beautiful islands arching across the South Pacific. Their white sand shores brush against lush green trees. The sun-sparkled waves lap the shoreline. The string of islands is called an *archipelago*. And in time, the islands are packaged into tours, and people, desiring this good thing, finding it a delight for the eyes, swarm to the archipelago with tubes of #9 sunscreen oil clutched in their eager hands.

Now imagine another archipelago, except that it is a string of prison camps stretching across interior Russia from Leningrad to the White Sea. This string of islands, this archipelago, is called the *Gulag*. Here in the Gulag the islands are strung over remote, barren terrain, far from any sandy shores, far from any packaged tours.

People come here, nonetheless. They arrive carrying not bottles of sunscreen oil but . . . nothing. Nothing but the clothes on their backs. They have been arrested during the night, too tired and shaken to ask *Why?* They are herded onto trains for the long trip to the islands. Perhaps they have asked the wrong question. Perhaps the local police had a quota to fill. Perhaps . . . perhaps. Without reasons they are sent on tour to work until they drop dead over their tools.

Here in the Gulag Archipelago the eternal Siberian blizzards rage. Theoretically, the prisoners are not supposed to work outside when the temperature hits sixty below. *Sixty below zero!* But every day they trudge out to work sites, heads muffled in fleabitten caps, the clothes they wear reduced to rags flapping in the Arctic winds about their gaunt bodies, the shoes replaced by pieces of rubber tires bound to their feet with wire. They march out to labor eight, ten, sixteen hours a day, felling trees for lumber, digging trenches for canals. They fall with the trees. They lie down and die in the canals, their bodies moved aside in the rubble of rock. The sides of the canals are patched with human corpses.

Disease rages in the camps—the islands of this archipelago— where the prisoners, who don't even know why they are on this tour, try to exist on seven or eight ounces of bread and a few cups of water a day. Illnesses wrack the prisoners so that some have to crawl to the work site on hands and knees. The skin erupts and blackens from poor diet and infections. The skin lies in gaunt folds over the bones. In the morning, the woman on the bunk above you may not get up. She has frozen, and the guards carry her stiff form like a log out to a shallow grave. In the summer the thawing earth emits the stench of death—from sixty million burials. The whole land is a charnel house.

And who knew about *this* archipelago that existed during all the Stalin years—and still exists today! Where did they advertise in glossy brochures for *tours?* This archipelago was packaged *out* of the public eye, never coming to light until Aleksandr Solzhenitsyn, a survivor, wrote of it beginning in 1956. *1956!* A time of peace and prosperity in the West, when vacationers sailed to distant islands to lie in the sun and listen to the rhythmic lapping of the waves.

Thus we wander east of Eden in pursuit of our own desires,

packaging the things we like, and those we don't like, into neat little nuggets. That road we wander chokes with brambles and snares to seduce humanity into believing it the right way, the only way. But not the Christian way. Left behind is the quiet garden where one might walk with God in the cool of the evening. Not with pretty packages, to be sure, because there has been only one gift ever given that makes the way *back* to Eden— to walking with God—possible. And the gift was not altogether lovely. This is how Isaiah describes it:

> He was despised and rejected by men;
>   a man of sorrows, and acquainted with grief;
> and as one from whom men hide their faces
>   he was despised, and we esteemed him not.
>   Isaiah 53:3

A few years ago a book was published, and gained national attention, on how to influence others by postures of power. We can change the way we sit, the way we talk, the way we gesture, the author argued, in order to wield power over others. Why would anyone want to do this? Because we are afraid of letting our real selves show. We're afraid of being hurt. Therefore, we should strike the first blow with a "package" of power.

A terrible danger lurks behind such packaging, a danger for human personality but more particularly for Christian living. Consider that extreme position: the posture of power. What happens to the biblical ideal of servanthood? Is this the model of Jesus, the one who was wounded for our transgressions and bruised for our iniquities? Jesus had power, surely. He said of himself, "All authority in heaven and on earth has been given to me" (Matt. 28:18). And yet, in his power, he chose to become the meekest of men, giving himself to the powers of his age—which he could have destroyed at the flick of a hand—for this reason only: that we may be free from sin. And, incidentally, from the need for packaging.

In a very real sense, packaging is an effort to hide our real selves and our sins, and it is from this effort that Jesus frees us. The power Jesus wielded, the power he exercised for us on the cross, was a liberating power that strips off our masks and frees us to be ourselves as God made us. In that lies true power—the power of Jesus in our lives, a living power that bears fruit in our lives as we walk in the way of Christian living back to the Eden of communion with God.

Fruit of the regenerated spirit cannot be packaged. It has to be free to grow outward and develop. In the lives of believers, those who wish to walk in the way of Christian living, spiritual fruits must be nurtured and liberated. This process, sometimes accompanied by painful pruning, sometimes joyfully liberated into full growth, we consider in this book.

For Discussion

We don't know what lies inside a package until we open it and expose it to the light. We do well to recognize the packaging we have made of our own fruit, and how best to expose the fruit to the light where it may grow.

Perhaps you have had a birthday party where you received a large gift, only to discover within the large package a smaller one, and so on—package within package. Often the gift finally disclosed is a small one—but valuable. One can't see the value of that gift until the packaging is torn away. In the same way, the fruit of the spirit may start as a small seed, buried under packages that must be torn away for the seed to grow in value and significance.

Sometimes we get comfortable with keeping that fruit packaged. It can take some daring to begin to strip away the packaging to see what lies inside. As a first step toward identifying spiritual fruits, however, begin by naming and listing the packagings that shield these fruits from life. Biblical guidelines may be found in the book of Ecclesiastes, especially 4:8; 5:10; 6:2; 6:9; and 7:10. One writer expressed the theme of vanity in Ecclesiastes like this: "If I lost everything I have, what would I have?"

CHAPTER TWO

The Christian Fruit

When I was a boy, not so very long ago, several times a week the still air along Neland Avenue was punctuated by the cry of the fruit and vegetable man. "Vegals, ho! Vegals, fresh fruit!" Then came the creak and groan of the heavily laden wagon and the clashing of the horse's hoofs against the tar pavement as the load drew heavily up the hill. Again, louder, the call broke the morning air: "Vegals! Fresh fruit!" And housewives, including my mother, would walk leisurely outside, rubbing hands on the apron each one wore, talking and laughing with one another. The young boys would admire the shaggy-shouldered horse as it drooped in its harness, or observe in wonder its huge, yellowed teeth. Sometimes the horse had a nose bag of grain draped on. In colder weather the horse bellowed huge clouds of steam.

Above all, I recall the glorious array of fruit and vegetables lined on the shelves of the ponderous wagon. The vegetable man had a small scale on the back of the wagon to weigh the housewives' selections. Huge branches of celery and onions. Heads of cauliflower so large they looked like basketballs. Brussel sprouts still embedded on thick stalks. If he had fresh apples he would break one into two neat halves with his bare hands to show how firm they were. He gave the pieces to the wondering boys—what power in those hands to snap an apple in half in one sharp twist!

The women would stand and chat with bunches of vegetables dangling in their arms. If the day was particularly hot, someone would bring iced tea and cookies for the vendor. He sucked this noisily under his full moustache. I remember that we always thought he looked a bit like his horse; but I remember best those neat mounds of fruits and vegetables riding the tiers of his wagon. It was a carnival of produce celebrated weekly.

7

Once a month or so, the vendor would make the rounds in his wagon, the large horse clashing steamily up the hill as always, but this time the wagon would have its tiers removed. The cry changed: "Rags, ho! Rags." In the wagon bed a litter of washed-out rags lay like fallen clouds.

How different it is today—and that scene was not so very long ago. Only rarely do we find produce stacked without packaging. And nowhere do we hear that haunting cry "Fresh fruit! Vegals, ho!"—a cry that brings us closer to the agricultural community of Jesus' time. The concept of the spiritual fruit is an analogy: a divine principle *rooted* in physical reality.

Jesus' teaching is always marked by its relevance to the immediate lives of the people he taught, and he often draws some analogy from the lives of the people that directs them toward spiritual understanding. In his use of this method, Jesus differs dramatically from most ancient teachers and philosophers, including those of the Hebrew nation. Those others generally began with some abstract concept and attempted to make it clear to the people. Plato begins with the idea of justice, Aristotle with logic and categories, the Pharisees and Sadducees with the law. Jesus begins with the real, daily lives of the people, for he is the "Emmanuel," the God with us, and as such he shows how our lives, rather than just our thinking, can be different.

The people Jesus taught were common laborers—fishermen, homemakers, farmers, and tradesmen. The Jewish nation as a whole was knit together by agriculture, for their society depended heavily upon grains and fruits of the earth. Wheat was prized for baking, barley generally the crop of poorer people. Olives were eaten fresh and pickled but most often were crushed for oil used for cooking and for lamp fuel. Grapes were eaten fresh, dried as raisins, or crushed for wine, a drink as normal for the people then as milk is for people today. Other important fruit crops included dates, figs, and almonds.

Jesus spoke to the people of this culture on their own terms. Of the forty parables of Jesus recorded in the New Testament, fully a third are related to agriculture in some way. When Jesus spoke of the sower and the different kinds of soil (Matt. 13:3-8), the people immediately saw the relevance of his teaching to their own lives. When he spoke of the mustard seed, the farmers understood its significance as readily as a modern farmer would understand contour farming as an analogy for keeping one's spiritual life on course. And what farmer wouldn't understand the necessity of pruning the fig tree in the parable recorded in Luke 13:6-9? One appreciates the exasperation of the farmer as the fig tree fails to bear its expected crop; one understands his desire to save the tree by nurturing it and pruning it; one understands, finally, that if the tree fails to bear fruit it *must* be cut down. In one neat little portrait, Jesus teaches the enduring lesson of faith and salvation.

Because these teachings are so thoroughly grounded in the lives of the people, they acquire relevance and urgency. No farmer is going to do nothing about an unbearing fig tree. His livelihood depends upon it. He will do everything in his power, and do it soon, to make the tree yield fruit. So, too, the relevance and urgency of faith is demonstrated in the parable.

While Jesus used many parables directly related to farming and fruit bearing, the language of fruit bearing enters his discourse with the ease and directness of one who both knows the people and loves them. Nothing reveals the tenderness and humility of Jesus quite so much as his recorded discourses. If we had no record of the words Jesus spoke, we might think of him as one of the aloof, lofty philosophers of ancient times. But the historical record in the Gospels indicates quite the opposite. His words are wise in their very simplicity, their tenderness, and their lovingkindness. Jesus spoke to the people as a friend. A friend speaks to his friends to build up—not tear down; to encourage—not discourage; to make his love clear—not to confuse and mystify. The very names by which Jesus reveals himself to his friends—"the bread of life," "the living water," "the good shepherd"—make him clearer and dearer to those friends.

One of the clearest passages of Scripture that ties together Jesus' teachings about his own nature, the way of Christian living, and the daily life of the people appears in John 15, where Jesus calls himself "the True Vine." The true vine is the central, life-supporting vine of the grape plant. It is the one from which all the others, the "trailers," draw sustenance and meaning. It defines and shapes all the other vines that depend upon it for life itself. But those vines are not merely "hangers-on." They must bear *evidence* of being a part of the main vine, and they do so, Jesus says, by bearing fruit. This is the evidence of being united to the True Vine. And those that do bear fruit, Jesus says, are pruned so that they "may bear more fruit." They are not expected to be static, producing a few little berries each year. They are expected to grow and to flourish into abundant life.

Jesus makes the analogy explicit. One imagines him standing by a grapevine with his disciples, then turning to them to make his point absolutely clear. "Abide in me," he says, "and I in you." Our lives are one. "As the branch cannot bear fruit by itself, unless it abides in the vine, neither can you, unless you abide in me." Making the analogy still clearer, Jesus says specifically to the disciples, "I am the vine, you are the branches. He who abides in me, and I in him, he it is that bears much fruit, for apart from me you can do nothing." And Jesus concludes with a warning drawn directly from the real life of the farmer but equally applicable to spiritual life: "If a man does not abide in me, he is cast forth as a branch and withers; and the branches are gathered, thrown into the fire and burned" (John 15:4-6).

This is the great blessing and the terrible reality of Christian living. It is a threefold process of fruit bearing. Grafted into Jesus as the True Vine, the Christian is expected to bear fruit. The life of the Christian needs pruning in order to bear abundant fruit. If the Christian doesn't bear fruit, his branch withers and is doomed.

Jesus foresees the trials that await his disciples, saying in John 16:1 that "I have said all this to you to keep you from falling away." He wants our branches to be strong and fruitful so that we may know the joy of life abundant, and pruning is one way to this life.

Be careful of pruning. It is a dangerous thing. We think of pruning as an action we do to something else. That bush, that plant—those things we prune. But now we are called to turn the razor-sharp blades on ourselves, and they will hurt.

As I write these very lines, here in the comfort of my study, the hot cup of coffee within reach, the pen moving easily over the white paper, I still have in my mind an uneasy darkness. This day, in preparation for a talk I must give to scholarship winners at the college where I teach, I have also finished studying the 1,960 page report of the Attorney General's Commission on Pornography (1986).

I have not led a sheltered life, and I do not consider myself a prude, but this report unnerved me. As a teacher of literature and a writer, I have an interest in censorship issues, the very reason I was initially led to the report. As I turned those many pages, I was drawn into a recognition of a violent and deranged world. Yet, unbelievably, many argue that pornography is only an issue of censorship. Witness Robert Yoakum writing in the *Columbia Journalism Review* (Sept.-Oct. 1986): "It is tempting to laugh off the Attorney General's Commission on Pornography. The zany field trips in search of smut, the endless and futile efforts to define pornography, the pretense that what it recommended wasn't censorship, all provided abundant material for editors, columnists, and cartoonists to ridicule the commission and its report. But while it is easy to guffaw at this federal farce . . . the comedy of errors has a darker side." That darker side, according to Yoakum, is that we have a right to this stuff. He concludes, "The U.S. is by no means the only country in which sexual and political censorship go hand in hand. . . . The specific lesson for journalists is that censors are censors are censors. And a free press must stoutly oppose them whether they come garbed as commissars, clerics, or clowns."

The commissioners, whose political leanings spanned the range from liberal to conservative, saw the issue otherwise. We cannot afford advocacy of freedom of the press and personal behavior at *any* cost, for the reality is that the price being asked is human lives and our perception of what it means to be human. Chairman Henry Hudson wrote that "The depictions . . . de-emphasize the significant natural bond between sex and affection. [The] material appears to impact adversely on the family concept and its value to society." Panel member Diane Cusack wrote, "People who consistently use the materials we have studied . . . are not made better persons for it. No pornographer has ever made that claim. And those who insist that these materials do no harm had better be right, for the risks to our future are substantial." She goes on to describe pornography as an abuse of humans to satisfy the perverse cravings of some. Panel member James Dobson, who reported on the findings in his *Focus on the Family* magazine, described the brutal murder of a young boy and wrote that "My knees buckled and tears came to my eyes as hundreds of other photographs of children were presented."

Pornography insults humanity, objectifying people as things and portraying sexuality as self-gratification upon objects. Where are the limits? In the dark world of pornography there are none, as this report painfully makes clear. Children are vilified, lured into sexual encounters and dispensed with like last night's garbage. Women become objects of brutal assault, their bodies mistreated and mutilated in ways we wouldn't treat animals. Here is the dark world, the perverse world, where the good thing of human sexuality is twisted beyond recognition.

How do they get away with it? In the surface world, the slick magazines like *Playboy* and *Penthouse* spend millions of dollars, since they are socially accepted, to wage the legal battles in the courts that permit the underworld of pornography to operate. *Christianity Today* reports that the Council for Periodical Distributors has set aside a war chest of $900,000 for the sole purpose of discrediting the report.

We would probably have little difficulty gaining agreement among Christians that pornography is a blight upon our nation and upon human nature that should be pruned out of existence. We would be better people without it. But is that the end of the matter for a Christian people? On the one hand, we have to root out links between immorality in our own lives and this flagrant immorality of pornography. But on the other hand, we also have to understand the joy of the Christian view of human sexuality, to recognize that this is a sacred gift given to humanity by which we express both physical and spiritual love. The marriage relationship—the only biblically condoned basis for sexuality—is the primary image used in the Bible to demonstrate the relationship between Christ and his bride, the church.

This twofold understanding also forms the pattern in this matter of pruning, as we shall see in the next chapter. Pruning is not just a matter of hacking out unwanted growth. It is also a matter of enabling spiritual growth, of enabling us to understand ourselves freely and fully as children of the most high Lord.

For Discussion

Nurturing the fruit of the spirit may be compared to traveling the Christian way that God has set for us by walking in his will. Read the first ten verses of Proverbs 2. What do these verses say about choosing the way of wisdom?

Notice that verses 1, 3, and 4 all contain conditional clauses. The conclusion from these conditions appears in verse 5. What are the conditions and the conclusion?

The following five verses give the results of accepting this conclusion. What are the results?

Notice that in verse 4 we are told to search for wisdom as we would for hidden treasure. Anyone who has made a treasure map as a child will understand that figure of speech. But suppose you found actual treasure using that map. How is the Bible a map to the treasure of wisdom?

What does verse 7 mean when it says that the Lord "is a shield to those who walk in integrity"?

CHAPTER THREE

Pruning through Uprooting

Reconciled to an inability to purchase expensive baubles, I have therefore delighted in being a lifelong collector of precious junk.

For example, when the cherry tree in which I used to climb as a boy was chopped down, I claimed a twisted section of its trunk for a coffee table, a piece probably not worth the ten coats of varnish needed to hide its fallen nature. Yet it reminds me of June mornings when the sun caught in the tree's branches and brushed ten thousand crimson globes. This was a tree that bore fruit, mind you. Not a few stray sprays of cherries, but bunches so thick that two hands were needed to pick them.

Occasionally, when the hours are late, the children are bedded, and stillness at long last has a chance to linger in the house, the grain of the wood seems almost to speak to a willing ear. Its cracked wooden throat etches whispers in the room, whispers of easy springs and hard winters, of proud youth and old age that twists the limbs and gnarls the grain, of wind-tossed times and gentle days. I am glad I have kept it.

"Something there is," wrote Robert Frost, "that doesn't love a wall"; but something there is in me that loves fences, even boughs of a cherry tree that fence in a patch of day for the human spirit to revel in. And I guess that is why I prize my precious junk—because I have made it mine and priceless by the very collecting. There I have fenced in a place, called it mine, and marked it as sacred.

My collecting has taken on other forms—that is, with an eye toward gain. Such attempts have come to a providential dead-end. Walking home with some boyhood friends one day, we were picked up by what we then called the local "hood," who nonetheless piloted a beautiful convertible. His arm muscles rippled from the trembling steering wheel up through several embarrassing tattoos to a T-shirt sleeve neatly tucked around a package of Camels humped up on the bulge of his shoulder. His hair glowed with the deep shine of Butch Wax, each black strand glued neatly in place as the wind tore past the windshield. The radio blatted out a song of which I caught snatches above the squeal of tires whining in terror. The song was called "Blue Moon of Kentucky," cut on the Sun label by Elvis Presley, at the time one more young "hood."

Thus, I became acquainted with precious junk of another sort. A year later I had procured the four records Elvis made on Sun label, before Colonel Parker steered him into the more lucrative RCA label. This was the singer who graduated from high school majoring in shop and English—and managed to render one of the most brutal massacres upon the latter in recorded history. I wrapped the four Sun label records in a brown paper bag and put them away in the attic. I knew a musical voice when I heard it, even when the voice was only minimally musical. But that was a merit in the '50s. About fifteen years later I looked for the bag and discovered that its questionable character had led to its being tossed out during that festival known as Spring Cleaning. I read in the paper one Friday night that a woman in Texas sold her Sun label copies for $7,500 apiece.

Well, I am thereby preserved from greed. But, also, I have become aware that there is some precious junk in our lives we do well to clean out, however valuable it seems at the moment.

Pruning is the hard, merciless thing to do. One always hopes for transformation, is reluctant to hack out the blighted or constricting branch. Any farmer, any backyard gardener, knows this feeling.

That branch of the rose with the mottled leaves—maybe if I let it go it will improve. But letting the blight of black-leaf have its own way impoverishes not just the one rose but all the others in the garden.

And that Althea bush, or "Rose of Sharon" as it's so nicely called—how can one cut out that profusion of growth, the dozens of feeder sprouts, that seem to promise such health and abundance?

And then too that tomato plant—every branch seems to promise fat red fruit. How can one snip off those tiny sprouts around the lower stalk that just might lead to the prize tomato?

And yet, if nothing else, experience teaches us that unchecked black-leaf blight will devastate the summer's roses, that those dozens of sprouts on the Althea suck out nourishment like leaches and rob the plant of its glorious bouquet of flowers, and that those vigorous young sprouts at the base of the tomato will diminish the August crop. And so we cut and prune for a healthier crop, even though it hurts so much at first.

Pruning of the fruit occurs in two ways. The first is a deliberate act of the farmer to rid the plant of those things he knows will ultimately destroy or diminish the crop. The analogy Jesus draws in John 15 is clear—the Christian must prune his life of the things that will destroy or diminish his fruit of the spirit. In short, the Christian must uproot, prune away, excise sin—what St. Paul calls the desires of the flesh. But there is a second, more subtle kind of pruning that arises from our living in a sinful world in which certain trials befall us that may either ultimately destroy or strengthen our Christian faith. We often wonder why bad things happen to good people. How can everything be all right when everything's going all wrong? We will look more closely at the second kind of pruning in the next chapter, but consider here the active pruning that the Christian must do, mercilessly and deliberately, with what we might call a kind of "cruel mercy," in order to develop his fruit.

Paul is very specific about the sins that must be pruned in the fifth chapter of Galatians, though this is not an exhaustive list of the weeds that have to be removed from the garden. There is in fact a subtle temptation here. If we stack our spiritual inventory against Paul's list and find ourselves free of, say, eight of the fifteen works he mentions, we might be tempted to consider ourselves in pretty good spiritual shape. Actually Paul's list is amazing in its scope, calling for a thorough overhaul of all areas in our life. Notice also that this must be done before the fruits may flourish. Paul says that "the desires of the flesh are against the Spirit" (Gal. 5:17); one cannot have the full fruit while the desires of the flesh remain. Not weeded out, these desires will overwhelm the garden of our spiritual lives.

The dandelion is a most efficient weed. It spreads broad leaves out from its base to choke off surrounding grasses. The giant taproot can cut down a foot into the ground to leach every nutrient and drop of water out of it. A homeowner seeing his lawn give way bit by bit to this weed, seeing the lovely yellow heads of the dandelions change to fluff that fills the yard and makes him sneeze every time he steps outside, might decide to do something about it, like stabbing a blade down around the root and jerking the plant out. But if that is his remedy, he will find to his dismay that a month later the familiar leaves will again be creeping dizzily over the yard. The dandelion has to be removed to the very bottom of its long and clinging root. If one little kernel of root is left, it begins methodically working its way back to the surface, where it will again choke out the good growth. Partially uprooted dandelions seem to come back stronger than ever.

The works of the flesh must be rooted out to the bottom. Jesus gave the best example when he taught the disciples about the one unclean spirit cast out of a man. If the man does not thoroughly root it out and replace it with the living spirit, the fruit of the spirit, the vacant space will be filled worse than ever: "Then he [the unclean spirit] goes and brings with him seven other spirits more evil than himself, and they enter and dwell there; and the last state of that man becomes worse than the first" (Matt. 12:45).

But where do we start? The list Paul offers (as a starting point?) in Galatians 5 is so lengthy and intimidating. Notice that each of them, however, is a manifestation of general human nature. In fact, the list may be conveniently broken down into human psychological and spiritual behaviors in five broad categories.

Fornication, impurity, and licentiousness are all kinds of *immorality*. Idolatry and sorcery are desecrations of spiritual allegiance to God Almighty, a violation of the first commandment, which enjoins us to have no other gods before Jehovah, and thus both constitute forms of *blasphemy*—denying the one true God by serving other gods. Enmity and strife are *social evils,* failures to live in peace and harmony with others, failures to love our brother and sister as ourself. Anger, selfishness, dissention, and envy are *emotional or psychological traits,* failures to live at peace with ourselves. Finally, the party spirit, drunkenness, and carousing form a *behavioral pattern,* a failure to represent ourselves to others as truly redeemed people of God. Notice, then, that Paul provides five general, personal areas in which we must weed our spiritual gardens to provide room for spiritual fruit. And if, as Paul says, the fruits of the spirit are counterparts to the works of the flesh, we observe also the counterpart from Galatians.

Weed	Human Dimension	Counterpart Fruit
Fornication Impurity Licentiousness	Immorality	Goodness
Idolatry Sorcery	Blasphemy	Faithfulness
Enmity Strife Jealousy	Social	Love Joy Kindness
Anger Selfishness Dissention Envy	Emotions	Peace Patience Gentleness (Meekness)
Party Spirit Drunkenness Carousing	Behavior	Self-Control

When I first started gardening, I did it with a deliberation that both amused and astounded my wife and friends. As early as November I amassed seed catalogs (quite literally, a mass of them). By February, I had my orders placed, sometimes to a half-dozen different companies whose seeds for one particular vegetable or herb I thought superior. During winter months I made plans on sheets of paper for the garden layout—trellised vegetables here, marigolds spaced there to keep out certain bugs, and so forth, even down to a fence of old tin cans tied together to frighten off the rabbits and woodchucks that I would spot on the hillside as they greedily eyed the patch. Almost before the snow melted I was turning compost into the soil. The one thing I couldn't plan for was the weeds. They always came up, more regular than rain. Once I was out of town for a few days and returned to find my wife weeding in the garden. A sudden July rain had brought out the quackgrass with a vengeance. If it wasn't rooted up right away, the weeds would surely damage the crop that summer. My wife knew this. Like the poor farmer, I was out of town.

She gave me a good lesson there—and it wasn't just one for helping each other in a marriage. The lesson was this: the matter of pruning and weeding is *urgent.* Left alone, those weeds will choke the crop.

When we take inventory of our spiritual garden, it is good to bear two principles in mind. First, pruning and weeding are urgent tasks. They can't be delayed, however precious the junk in our lives seems to us. Second, they must be done thoroughly. Not even the kernel of the root must be left or, like the dandelion, the weed will spring back. We must apply ourselves constantly to this ongoing task, but the task will be simplified considerably if we recall Paul's instruction to give our lives a spiritual inventory in areas of morality, true worship of God, social relationships, emotions, and behavior.

Still we ask *How?* How can I uproot the weed that chokes the fruit? First, we must recognize it as a sin. A gardener who can't tell a weed from a vegetable sprout won't have much success at harvest. We have to identify the weeds. Second, we have to confess the sin as a step toward separating ourselves from it. The act of identifying it as *something we don't want* is comparable to the physical weeding of a garden. Third, we ask Jesus to forgive the sin. We remind ourselves that Jesus didn't die to save perfect people; he died to save sinners. We must claim that forgiveness, recognizing as we do so that Jesus' forgiveness did not *end* at Calvary but endures until he comes again. And, fourth, we both praise Jesus for his forgiveness and nurture new spiritual growth to take the place of the weeds. This is where the fruits of the spirit enter: they make for a life of praise to God for the great things he has done at the same time they nurture our spiritual lives, helping us to be all that he wants us to be.

We must prune out the weeds in our lives, but we must also remember *why* we do it. It is to make us healthy. The fact that we have to prune the weeds in our lives doesn't mean we are thoroughly bad, miserable people. Pruning is always a way to health, the way to greater goodness, the way to rich fruit and abundant living. Pruning should be thorough—but gentle; it must be sure—but loving and full of hope.

For Discussion

The final chapter of the book of Acts reports that Paul was struck by a viper: "Paul had gathered a bundle of sticks and put them on the fire, when a viper came out because of the heat and fastened on his hand" (Acts 28:3). In a sense, sin is like the viper, and very much like weeds that have to be pruned from the garden of spiritual fruit.

What if Paul had simply pretended the viper was not real? It would have been a deadly mistake. Sin is as real and deadly as a viper, fastening its hook into our lives. Paul shook the creature off into the flames. It is necessary for us to identify the sins that fasten to us in order to shake them off into the flames.

You might consider doing this. Identify the sin or sins that have fastened themselves to you and jot their names on a piece of paper. Then burn that piece of paper. In a very real sense this is what Jesus did for us when he took our sins upon him on the cross.

CHAPTER FOUR

Pruning through Sorrow

We cannot leave a spiritual garden untended any more than we can leave a physical garden untended. But what about those times when the rains come in such torrents that the seed drowns? And what about those summers when the sun sears the parched earth and the wind beats the withered crop?

Because we live in a world that is fallen, bad things happen to good people. This is clearly not the will of the Father. God created *Eden;* not until humanity disobeyed God did we have to sweat and toil over the crop. God created humanity good; not until we turned from God to follow personal desires, to grow weeds instead of fruit, did we suffer sickness and pain.

These are hard words for the Christian life, not the soft, comforting words we wish we could hear. The first hard word is that to bear spiritual fruit we must prune the desires of the flesh. The second hard word is that in our walk through life, events beyond our control will prune and scar and cut us back, events that are going to hurt when we remember them.

We didn't understand many things about the event, the pruning through sorrow that I now recall. Every aspect of it appeared at the time like a rude surprise to further confound our grief.

The casket, for example. In cold, clinical terms it was off-white molded fiberglass resembling the worn marble tiles of certain cathedrals, but of a lustre never seen where the living walk. Its bed was twenty-four inches in length, and it came in two models—one with a satin bed and bare exterior, the other covered inside and out with a softly frocked linen. There was also a plain styrofoam box, not unlike a picnic cooler. The one chosen for this final bed was that with the linen frocking. Before it was lowered into the grave it would be covered with a fiberglass shell that would form an air bubble acting as a vault. This is the way it went with infant burials. There were a great many things we didn't know.

In all of time's turning, history doesn't prepare us for death. And how could you have dreamed it, my brother Tim and my sister-in-law Velda, with three healthy children and a fourth apparently so? There was no preparation: death sent no messages of warning, but simply crept in between the nine o'clock and eleven o'clock feedings. Rebecca, laid to rest warm and living, was picked up with the chill of death on her. You placed your lips on hers and tried to resuscitate her, your tears falling on her cold eyes, while the wail of sirens split the night.

"A people without history," wrote T. S. Eliot in *Little Gidding,* "is not redeemed from time, for history is a pattern / Of timeless moments." You had no history for this; but in all of time to be, that moment will return. It is timeless now, that time when time ended for Rebecca, born October 25, 1983, died December 25, 1983. Only two months of time comprise her history, yet there will not be a time when we look into each other's eyes, or shake hands, or give some other similar, small token by way of greeting, that we won't remember this time when we wept in each other's arms.

Born October 25, 1983, Rebecca died December 25, 1983. Those are the hard, unforgettable words that coil into the tissue of the brain.

While struggling to write the obituary with the funeral director, we fumbled the words: "Rebecca Kay . . . went to be with the Lord. . . . No, say, went to be with Jesus, because it was Jesus' birthday." And that is the picture that cuts finally through the gray.

The cold December wind wailed out of the north like grief, gray snow pelting and drifting in the streets, in the cemetery, three feet of snow on the ground and the temperature hovering around zero for the third consecutive week.

There were only three cars, holding our entire family, at the cemetery. And the one who had left us, the youngest, Rebecca, lay in the station wagon that led us to this barren ground. An old tractor parked near a snowdrift marked the gravesite. We tried to walk in its tire tracks through the snow, cradling that small casket between us. When we arrived at the site we weren't sure what to do. The grave was so shallow, so small. The old man by the tractor asked if anyone had straps. No one did. And it was better that way, for, by getting down on our hands and knees in the snow and dirt by the grave, each holding an end of the suddenly heavy casket, we were able ourselves to lean down and lay Rebecca home.

We thought of that tiny, lonely little daughter inside the white fiberglass, dressed in the pink sleeper that had been her Christmas outfit, her small hand fisted around a spray of pink rosebuds. We saw her there, while the gray sky spumed snow and the wind wailed at the tears on our cheeks. It was Velda who said that when Rebecca rose to meet Jesus, she would be holding fresh roses in her hand to greet him.

How could we not weep, seeing that.

And with the wind whipping at my words as I tried to pray, we—those in the family who had to wait—stood around that tiny space beneath our feet, held hands, and said goodbye to Rebecca.

Our flower for two brief months, she flourished, blossomed, and then, within seconds during her sleep, died.

But another picture holds our minds. Two pictures. And they both came from a friend who, in the space of twenty minutes at the funeral service, opened a door on eternity for us so we can hold this timeless moment.

"Suppose," he said in that brief sermon, "that on October 25, 1983, you were given a new car, and that on December 25, 1983, it was demolished in an accident. You would be saddened, but it can never compare to your loss. Or suppose that on October 25 you were given a new house, and that on December 25 it burned to the ground. It would sadden you, but it can never compare to your loss. For Rebecca was a living child, a gift of God, a gift full of promise.

"I have knelt," he said, "by the crib of a young daughter—my own—and wondered how I could ever live without her. I have knelt by the bedside of a young son—my own—in the litter of Legos and toys, and wondered how I could ever bear not seeing him play with those toys again. . . ."

At his words, my mind jolted back to another Christmas two years before. I remember the time because I dated the letters I wrote that night . . .

I don't know what called me from my bed during the early morning hours of December 25, 1981. This in itself was not unusual. I have learned to give in to the thoughts that come creeping in between dreams during the night, give in to them and let them rouse me from sleep and walk me down to the study, the dog sniffing lazily at my heels hoping a marshmallow will drop from the hot chocolate or from my hand. She curls near my feet when I sit behind the desk in that absolute, still quiet of deep night, only her weary sighing and the faint scratching of the pen while I write disturbing the quiet. But the thoughts in my mind that night were strange ones. This was Christmas morning; why this sudden, vast loneliness?

"I have knelt by a child's crib—my own—and wondered what I would do or say if I should ever lose him."

I hold in my hand this letter, written December 25, 1981, to Jeffrey Todd, you who almost had another name.

We had been married nearly six years, your mother and I, when almost on impulse—but an impulse six years in the making—we dialed the phone number of the local Children's Services. Precisely nine months later we held you in our arms. But there was a mystery to it that those cold, factual words don't begin to suggest. For example, after the home surveys and the conferences and the interviews, the reality of having a child at last crept upon us. This would have been about the third month. It was then that we chose a name for our son: Bradley John. And so it remained. Until the day we received a call from the agency: Would you come by at 2:30 on Thursday?

Yes, of course. It gave us time to buy a crib, boxes of diapers, jars of food. Time to lose our own appetites, to go without sleep, to pace the floor nervously, to putter in the garden, to look at a book and not see the words.

And late that night, this:

"Suppose it's a girl," your mother said.

"It's supposed to be. They always say the first adoption is a girl. Then the spoiling won't hurt so much."

"Why may only girls be spoiled?"

"I don't know. If that's a word for love, it would be the same either way."

"Are you sure of the name?"

"Bradley John?"

"Yes."

"What do you suggest?"

"Jeffrey."

"Jeffrey Todd," I answered. And so it was. *Jeffrey* From the Teutonic, meaning "God's promise."

And at the agency that Thursday, December 2, 1971—we have the Polaroid photo in the front of your baby album, the young couple looking down into the brown eyes, holding the tiny, nine-week-old baby the director of the agency said, "The foster parents always give the children what we call a 'stage name,' until their own parents name them. It's not important now, but his stage name has been Bradley."

Jeffrey Todd: God's promise. This letter I gave you when you awakened that Christmas morning recounts only small tracks on the sands of time, the kinds of things a father recalls when he awakens during the night with the children sleeping soundly from much living, bits and pieces that only suggest the love a father bears for God's promise. The first camping trip we took alone when during the night your small hand reached over and found mine so that we fell asleep that way. The night when you were fearful, as all three-year-olds are, in your room and I overheard your mother comforting you:

"You know Jesus is with you."

A smile from you.

"You know God watches over you."

A smile and a nod.

"And you know God sends his angels to keep watch over you."

A pause, then, "You can keep those guys away from me."

I choked on my laughter in the hall.

Only eleven months after you came to us your first sister was born. It was a hard birth—mother developing allergies to the child within her, the hospitalization, the drugs that at once threaten and protect in that delicate symbiosis that typifies medicine.

You too, Betsy, "God's peace," have left tracks in the sands of time that I traced in my mind that night. A dozen of your pictures adorn my office walls. While turning the pages of a book, I suddenly find penned in a margin: "I love you. Betsy." Life with you is serendipity in pen and ink—a bouquet of designs and artwork on every wall, hung on the refrigerator door with magic-magnets, strewn on floors, overflowing drawers. But especially this I prize. It is on my study wall: a picture of a great, shuffling, brown bear wearing glasses and smoking a pipe, given to me while I was in the hospital briefly. And under the bear you penned these words: "Dear Dad. Even though you may be old, you're still great."

And your coming, Tamara, from the Hebrew for "twin," last of my children, I had to remember this lightening night of December 25, 1981, was not easy either. In fact, we thought you were one of two, but your brother or sister never developed. And as your mother was allergic to your older sister, it was only fair that you should be allergic to your mother. I remember the violet lights they laid you under after birth, the pallid gold of your skin, the terribly escalating bilirubin counts for days, the scheduling of a blood transfusion, and then the sudden miracle that let us take a healthy daughter home three days later.

The last flower in the garden blooms with a special sweetness, slender, lively. You were the only child who would fall asleep on my shoulder when I walked the living room with you. Maybe it was because my cracked singing had adjusted to a child's ear by then, but I like to believe it was the shoulder. You had an album of speech all your own: a love for "hangleburgs" at the restaurant, wanting to wear your hair in "cowtails." And the questions that never stopped, from wondering how big "deputy" was (even when we figured out that "deputy" meant "infinity," we were still at a loss for an answer) to wondering how there could still be snow in the high peaks of the Sierra Nevadas in July, which is when we stopped there for a playful snowball fight.

So eager to live, so full of life. Why then the fairy-like eagerness, the young gymnast who could do splits in a way that made your father grit his teeth, stretched out on the hospital bed at the age of four. The medical exactness of the surgery was intended to allay fear: open the chest with a lateral incision, cut the rib cage, reconstruct the split sternum with grafts and silver wire. A thorough restructuring to let the lungs find air for the gymnastics, to provide the heart room to pound through the heart-stopping splits. The surgeon said you would be able to wear a bikini and the scar wouldn't show. It was then that I began to cry—not for the pain you were about to bear, but for the loss I saw down the future when some newer lover would look upon you, and want you, and take you from me. "But I always want to live with you, daddy," you said.

I realized that even in our deepest moments of love, we are preparing each other for loss. Each moment of life is a moment of death, and we hold on tight and beg its delay.

This my children have taught me; this I paused to remember that night of December 25, 1981; this I remembered again that night of December 25, 1983, as this child, Rebecca Kay, lay surrounded by pink rosebuds waiting . . . waiting.

A second picture was stirred by the pastor's words.

"But God understands," he was saying. "This is also his loss, for, as Isaiah tells us, God knew Rebecca before she was knit in the womb. Her life is engraved on the palm of God's hand.

"But, in yet a deeper way God understands. You yourselves have said, 'Rebecca went to be with Jesus on Jesus' birthday.' And that is fitting, for on Jesus' birthday God lost *his* son. God stood on the threshold of heaven as we stand on the threshold of the grave and said goodbye to his son."

There it is; that old theological term *kenosis*, which there at the grave suddenly took on new meaning. God "emptied himself" through his son Jesus, took on the form of a servant, was born in the likeness of men. Even though he was rich, for our sakes he became poor, so that by his poverty we might become rich. There is the mystery of loss: the gulf between God's riches and Jesus' poverty, between our loss and Rebecca's wealth. While we weep by the grave in the keen December wind, she romps on the playgrounds of heaven. That is the gulf, and it is crossed only by death, because Jesus on the cross became the bridge.

In Eliot's "The Journey of the Magi," one of the Magi, bewildered by grace, dazed by divinity, reflects:

> Were we led all that way for
> Birth or Death? There was a Birth, certainly,
> We had evidence and no doubt. I had seen birth and death,
> But had thought they were different; this Birth was
> Hard and bitter agony for us, like Death, our death.

There are times when sorrow and grief hound us with the cruel baying of death. But that other Death, when on Christmas Day God bade farewell to his son, knelt by his grave as the Magi knelt by his cradle, is the joy which brings light to the darkness.

Sorrow is the hard pruning; none of us escapes it. It comes in different forms to different people. For some it is death, for others it is terrible loneliness, for others the bleakness of unrelieved depression. None of us escapes the seas of sorrow that engulf our lives. But the prophet Nahum tells us that God's "way is in whirlwind and storm. . . . He rebukes the sea and makes it dry" (Nah. 1:3-4). And Zechariah tells us that "his dominion shall be from sea to sea" (Zech. 9:10). During the times when sorrow seems to drown us, when bad things happen to good people, when the pruning shears seem to nip too close to the heart, the Christian can proclaim that God's way is in the sea, that God reigns, and that God will never forsake us.

For Discussion

I think we would all agree that the events that cause sorrow are bad things. But can the bad thing ever produce a good thing?

In the third and fourth chapters of Philippians, Paul teaches important lessons about dealing with suffering.

First, in Philippians 3:3, he testifies that we put our confidence in Jesus, not in the flesh. It is true that things of this world can fail us. We don't know what our lives will be like tomorrow. But we have confidence in the unchanging and loving Lord. We know what he will be like tomorrow.

Second, in 3:8 Paul says that the things that we lose in this life are not important if through them we gain Christ. Sometimes we lose things in order to be redirected to our need for Christ.

Third, notice the verbs in verses 12-15 of chapter three. They are active verbs. Even though we may face sorrow, we *press on,* we *strain forward* toward Christ. When sorrow weighs us down, we fix our strength and our goal in Christ.

Fourth, Paul gives his great summary in 4:5-7. If we are truly fixed on Jesus, we need not have any anxiety about anything. Paul tells us that the "peace of God, which passes all understanding, will keep your hearts and your minds in Christ Jesus."

CHAPTER FIVE

LOVE

Getting back to Bethel

Having considered the hard words—the pruning we must do to ensure the flourishing of our spiritual fruits, and the difficult events that befall us to test our faith—we are ready to consider the good words. And what good words they are: love, joy, peace, patience, kindness, goodness, faithfulness, gentleness, self-control. They are good words, Paul says, because "against such there is no law." They are words of freedom, words of life abundant, words that turn our mourning into dancing, our darkness into light.

Perhaps the very root of the vine that produces these good fruits is love, the primary fruit, the fruit that makes all the others possible and gives them meaning.

Dozens of books have been written on the subject of spiritual love, often intricately describing the different words used for love in Scripture—*agape*, divine love; *phileo*, friendship; *eros*, sensual love. To be sure, different kinds of love are described in Scripture, but love isn't to be neatly categorized in the life of the believer, for all love originates in our love for God and his love for us. Divine love is like the pebble thrown into a still pool. Without that first splash of the pebble striking water there is no action at all; but after the first splash the concentric rings spread out over the water until the entire surface ripples with action.

Divine love can't be understood first of all as an action; the actions follow from being *in* love—in God's love. From this *state of being*, which we call "the Christian walk," all other actions of love flow.

But neither does this suggest that being *in* love means we are inactive, or passive like a baby being held in its mother's arms.

Love is the first desire, the true vine bearing spiritual fruit, the primary nourishment for all other fruits, and it involves both being in God and acting in his will. Consider the analogy of the pebble in the pond. If that pond is stagnant and choked with growth, the rings of the pebble become tight little lines that fold in on themselves. One must imagine the pond nourished by the living, flowing water of Jesus, which clears away all that is dead and stagnant, making it possible for the ripples from the first pebble to ring outward and outward. To get a clearer idea of this *being in love* and *acting in love*, we have to turn first of all to the biblical patterns. Remember, however, that the Bible is not a philosophical treatise on love but a treasury of illustrations and examples of love. The greatest example, of course, is God's having become human in the person of Jesus. But God was not silent on the subject of love until this point. Indeed, his every act, from the first loving activity in creating humankind, is an act of love.

One example of a person who had to put himself in a relationship with the True Vine, the very source of love, is Jacob. In this great patriarch we see a pattern common to Old Testament heroes of faith—the man who strays from the Lord and finds everything going all wrong, the man who has to get back to Bethel, the altar of his love, before things can work out right.

Jacob was a conniver and a fighter. His father, Isaac, was forty when Rebekah became pregnant with twins—twins who struggled so fiercely within her that she wondered how she could go on living. This was more than "morning sickness" for the pregnant Rebekah; it was a foreshadowing of a lifelong struggle between "two nations in her womb," the nation of Esau and the nation of Jacob. And history bore out the prophecy.

The story of how Jacob tricked Esau out of his blessing, how he had to flee the land when Esau threatened to kill him, is a familiar one. Even as the aged Isaac sent Jacob on his way, he bestowed the blessing of Abraham upon him: he would be the father of the promised people upon whom God's favor would rest. It must have seemed anything but God's favor as Jacob fled the land into the wilderness, his brother's wrath a hot goad at his back.

Then Jacob came to a place where he had a vision in which God affirmed his love. Jacob built an altar of stones, anointed them with oil, and called the place Bethel—"The House of God." This was the place where God had talked with him, where he had been enfolded in God's love and promise. But the journey continued.

For Jacob it was a journey of trials and frustrations: his back-breaking labor for Laban, his marriage to Leah and yearning for Rachel, and then having to flee again, this time from Laban, into the wilderness. His days were marked by wandering. Reconciliation came with Esau, but even in the reconciliation his own family created problems. His daughter Dinah was taken by Shechem the Hivite, and battle broke out against his enemies. His family turned to idols. What had happened to the promises?

It was time for renewal, time to walk again in his first love for God, to rely on his promises alone. God appeared to Jacob and told him to get back to Bethel, to enter again the "House of God." Jacob journeyed in spiritual renewal to Bethel, where once again he could speak to God and find the promises renewed.

The story of Jacob forms a familiar pattern in the Old Testament, and indeed for the children of God in the Israelite nation. Over and over they turned from the source of love to go their own way; over and over again God called them back to Bethel and renewed his promises to them. The love of God doesn't change. It is the still point in the storm of life.

Surely God grieves over the waywardness of his children; he is a loving parent. But always he waits with arms open. This truth became the primary subject of the prophets, who affirm several key principles about spiritual love that are reaffirmed in the New Testament.

The task of the prophets was twofold: to declare the wrongdoings or errors of the age and to point to the higher way of the Lord God. Ultimately this higher way is the prophecy of the coming Messiah. So too, in matters of love we find the prophets declaring that certain weeds in the spiritual garden must be uprooted, and then pointing to the higher love of God that is ultimately incarnated in Jesus.

The prophets lived in a time of political unrest and chaos for the chosen people. During this time the people of God turned from the living word of God to the words of an unsettled world. Repeatedly the prophets tried to turn them from following their own will to following the way of God, often specifying their sins that lay contrary to love. In this spirit Isaiah declares the word of God: "For I the Lord love justice, I hate robbery and wrong" (Isa. 61:8). One cannot walk in God's love when one violates God's justice—a theme that is echoed by later prophets. Amos calls the people to "Hate evil, and love good, and establish justice in the gate" (Amos 5:15). "Let justice roll down like waters, and righteousness like an overflowing stream," says Amos (5:24). Justice is a bedrock of spiritual love. Micah, too, echoes the call: "What does the Lord require of you but to do justice, and to love kindness, and to walk humbly with your God?" (Mic. 6:8). Zechariah, like the others, calls us to "love truth and peace" (Zech. 8:19).

The word is clear throughout the prophets. One cannot walk in spiritual love unless one is just and honest. The theme is too large in the Old Testament to ignore. But opposed to the love of men, which is too often prone to the weeds of strife, envy, and selfishness, is the love of God the Father. Note the qualities of *this* love that are established in the Old Testament.

God's love is an everlasting love. Unlike the fickle nature of human love, which changes allegiances according to the desires of the flesh, God's love remains unchanged from age to age. His love is eternal, decreed to us from before the beginning of time and still there for us when time ends in the kingdom where God's hand "will wipe away every tear from their eyes" (Rev. 21:4). In the unsettling transitions of the Hebrew nation, Jeremiah spoke the reassuring word of God to them: "I have loved you with an everlasting love; therefore I have continued my faithfulness to you" (Jer. 31:3). What an assurance this is—that God's love is *never* absent.

God's love reaches out. The eleventh chapter of Hosea is one of the great passages on God's love, establishing the fact that God's love reaches out to us, that his almighty and loving arms are spread wide to receive us when we turn to him. But it is also a passage of unforgettable sadness. While God's love is everlasting, human love is not. Thus Hosea's word of the Lord begins in grief: "When Israel was a child, I loved him." God points out his steadfast lovingkindness to Israel. But faced with the infidelity and waywardness of human love, the question is raised, "Shall the people be forsaken as they have forsaken God?" And God responds, "How can I give you up, O Ephraim! How can I hand you over, O Israel" (v. 8). Instead, God declares that he will call out to his people with the roar of the lion. This prophecy is specifically fulfilled in the Messiah to come, described in the book of Revelation as "the lion of Judah." Jesus is God's call to his people, his reaching out with arms of love to receive his people.

God's love is a haven, a resting point. If God's love is, first of all, everlasting, and, second, if it reaches out to his wayward people, then a third principle we see in God's love is that it provides a secure haven in which the loved ones can rest. One of the great longings of our fast-paced age is for security, for something that doesn't change when everything else does. In Robert Frost's well-known poem "The Death of the Hired Man," a character says, "Home is the place where, when you have to go there, / They have to take you in." What a cold and bitter view! To have to take someone in! God owes us no such responsibility. He doesn't *have* to take us in. Yet he has prepared a place for us in his arms and eagerly awaits our return. The prophet Zephaniah promises this peace: "The Lord, your God, is in your midst, a warrior who gives victory; he will rejoice over you with gladness, he will renew you in his love" (Zeph. 3:17). God will renew us; he has prepared a haven for us to rest in. At the very doorstep to his haven, he removes from us the weight of our worries and our sins. He casts them, as Micah says, "into the depths of the sea" because of his steadfast love. This is love beyond our human comprehension, but more incomprehensible still is the love manifested by God's sending his son Jesus to incarnate physically these great, divine principles of spiritual love.

Thus the prophets affirm at least three great principles of the spiritual fruit of love. It is an *everlasting* love, a love that doesn't change from day to day but endures despite the changes in the one who is loved. Some people are hard to love. They can only be described as unlovely. Yet spiritual love steadfastly bestows love upon them. Second, the spiritual fruit of love *reaches out* to others. It doesn't wait until they may wander our way but gives them a way to our love. And, third, spiritual love provides a *haven*. It restores the soul and affirms one's worth. It provides rest.

These principles that the prophets give us in the Old Testament are active and emphatic because they come from the Lord himself. They are the essential starting point to developing our spiritual fruit of love. But wait a minute, one might say. Hasn't God also given specific commands about love? Indeed he has, and the truly remarkable thing, as we shall see in the next chapter, is how both the principles and the commands are fulfilled in the person and teachings of Jesus.

For Discussion

An easy trap is laid for Christians when we begin to discuss the weeds that grow in the lives of non-Christians. For example, what is the opposite of love? Is it simply hatred? Is it sufficient to contrast hatred to the fruit of love in the Christian life? Perhaps we should consider the areas of our lives in which we have failed to show genuine Christian love. There is a distinction here between the exact opposite to love, which is hatred, and failing to love as we ought.

But it is also important in our Christian life to recognize the positive growth. Ask this question: In what one area of my life have I shown love during the past week, or month, or year? How can I show love to someone today? It may be our aim in the way of Christian living to live in the full joy of Jesus' love, but too often we fail to appreciate the positive steps we make along that way. Too quickly we focus on the negative in our lives. We do well at times to compile our own positive spiritual inventory as a guide along the way of Christian living.

CHAPTER SIX

LOVE
From Bethel to Bethlehem

At the heart of Christianity is Christ; at the heart of God's love is
Jesus—the one who makes human love possible and the one who
provides the model for human love. Jesus himself said, "Think
not that I have come to abolish the law and the prophets; I have
come not to abolish them but to fulfil them" (Matt. 5:17). In no
way is this fulfillment better exemplified than in spiritual love.

In the preceding chapter we considered certain principles of
love established by the prophets—that love is everlasting, that
love reaches out, that love is a haven. Each of these we see
fulfilled in Jesus. But how did Jesus also fulfill the law, the
commandments declared to Old Testament people?

The commandments of God are never simply a list of "shalt
nots," of things we shouldn't do. The law is always bracketed by
two great and positive commandments. The first of these is to
love God. In Deuteronomy 6:5, God, through Moses, tells the
Israelites his divine purpose in giving the law in the so-called
"law of love": "You shall love the Lord your God with all your
heart, and with all your soul, and with all your might." And the
so-called "great requirement" is given in Deuteronomy 10:12:
"What does the Lord your God require of you, but to fear the
Lord your God, to walk in all his ways, to love him. . . ."

How is Jesus the fulfillment of this commandment? First of
all, he is God's love incarnate. But he also makes this *active,
positive* principle of the law the chief commandment, the one
that gives meaning to all the others. The "shalt nots," which the
Pharisees multiplied beyond belief, offer a way of *avoiding* evil, a
way of pruning, we might say. But this commandment offers a
way to and a *way for* Christian living. When the Pharisees try to

trap Jesus by asking him which is the great commandment of the law, Jesus responds, "You shall love the Lord your God with all your heart, and with all your soul, and with all your mind" (Matt. 22:37). This is precisely the same law given by God in the Old Testament. But Jesus is *God*. His will does not change. His love is everlasting and his law is eternal. Therefore, Jesus declares "This is the great and first commandment."

But Jesus adds another principle (and here we see the true nature of the fruit of love): "And a second is like it, You shall love your neighbor as yourself. On these two commandments depend all the law and the prophets" (Matt. 22:39-40). This second law, of course, is also rooted in the Old Testament commandments that Jesus came to fulfill. We find it stated specifically in Leviticus 19:18 ("you shall love your neighbor as yourself"), but it runs as a steady, seamless thread through all the Old Testament law. Thus Jesus does fulfill the Old Testament law and prophets in his teaching. Spiritual love originates in love for God, but it doesn't stop there. It flows outward like concentric rings in a pool to all others who are our neighbors. And our neighbors, as Jesus demonstrated in his parable of the Good Samaritan, are all others on the face of the earth. So important is this principle to Jesus that it is implicit throughout his teaching repeatedly and often stated directly, as in his advice to the rich young ruler (Matt. 19:19).

The spiritual fruit of love begins, then, in love for God and immediately, instinctively reaches out in love for our neighbor. The question we bring to the life of Jesus, the question for which he supplies abundant answer, is this: How do we practice this "neighbor love" so important to the teaching and ministry of Jesus, so vital to our fruit of the spirit?

It may rightly be said that, as the fulfillment of God's Great Commandment, Jesus illustrates in every word and act the spiritual fruit of love. To compile a list of attributes of spiritual love would be no less daunting a task than to compile a list of attributes of Jesus himself. However, in a passage from the Gospel of John, Jesus meets with his disciples and tutors them by both word and action in the way of love. This is his final message to the ones he loved as friends and brothers, a message full of poignancy, grief, and promise—a message as enduring as all eternity.

The scene is the feast of the Passover. Jesus, who knows full well that these are his last hours before the crucifixion, has just made the triumphal entry into Jerusalem that triggers the events leading to Golgotha. Now he meets for a short time with his disciples and those closest to him.

A most curious thing happens as they prepare for the feast. Jesus knows the events about to unfold. He knows that Judas awaits the sign to betray him. As a kind of preface to his teachings in these final hours, particularly those on love, Jesus performs this remarkable act: he abases himself as a slave and washes his disciples' feet. The deed is preface for his words. In fact, Jesus calls the deed "an example, that you also should do as I have done to you" (John 13:15). Spiritual love, we conclude, divests itself of any superiority and begins in the humblest of actions. On the basis of this act, Jesus declares to his disciples: "A new commandment I give to you, that you love one another; even as I have loved you, that you also love one another" (v. 34). In a most dramatic and unexpected fashion the Lord of heaven and earth opens his heart to his disciples on the subject of the fruit of love.

One notes, first of all, that all the principles established by the prophets are affirmed by Jesus, but they are affirmed with special relevance and urgency. While the prophets spoke of God's everlasting love, we find the incarnation of God's love in Jesus: "God so loved the world that he gave his only Son, that whoever believes in him should not perish but have eternal life" (John 3:16). As such Jesus is the bridge to everlasting love, the bridge that crosses the chasm made by man's sin. In the Passover scene we're focussing on here, Jesus affirms this bridge of everlasting love: "As the Father has loved me, so have I loved you; abide in my love" (John 15:9). And Jesus adds that "I shall pray the Father for you" (John 16:26). This is indeed a unique bridge: not one on which we just ride across under our own power, but one that actually carries us to our final destination in everlasting love.

Moreover, Jesus affirms the prophetic principle that *love reaches out*. Indeed, with his insistence upon the second great commandment—that we love our neighbor as ourselves—Jesus emphasizes the principle of *active,* dynamic love. If we have a bridge through Jesus to the Father's everlasting love, it naturally follows that we build our bridges, on Jesus' foundation, to others. Thus Jesus provides his "new commandment": "that you love one another; even as I have loved you" (John 13:34). Here Jesus makes specific use of the analogy of spiritual fruit. "I am the true vine," he says in John 15:1, and, cautioning that God "the vinedresser" will prune away branches that bear no fruit, he specifically states that the disciples are his branches to bear the fruit of love for others. But Jesus is not just the pattern giver; he is the pattern itself. When he says of reaching out to others that "Greater love has no man than this, that a man lay down his life for his friends" (John 15:13), he provides the paradigm by which we measure the ways in which we give of our lives so that others may live.

No other spiritual principle bears such great contemporary urgency. While the world about us cries out in spiritual and physical hunger, how can we turn our back on the Savior's example? The urgency has not diminished since Jesus' day; it has only grown larger. Still, many of us spend our lives acquiring for ourselves. We lay down our lives in the office and are too tired or too busy or too unconcerned to realize the need of a perishing world. And it is so easy to justify that labor for ourselves. Don't we have an obligation to our family's comfort? Don't we have a duty to the church budget? Surely, but Jesus enjoins us to lay down our lives for our neighbor. No writer makes more forceful use of this principle than James, who calls it "the royal law." The beauty of James's writing lies in his practicality and concreteness, as when he asks "What does it profit, my brethren, if a man says he has faith but has not works?" (James 2:14). He immediately supplies the urgent response: "If a brother or sister is ill-clad and in lack of daily food, and one of you says to them, 'Go in peace, be warmed and filled,' without giving them the things needed for the body, what does it profit? So faith by itself, if it has no works, is dead" (James 2:15-17).

Those who exercise such Christian love call considerable scorn upon themselves. The world can well understand a person who lays down his life for a career; indeed, this is the world's standard for success. But someone who lays down his life in neighbor-love—this person the world calls a fool. Jesus recognized this. He himself was mocked and scorned for laying down his life for his friends. For those who follow his example, he acknowledges that "the world has hated them because they are not of the world, even as I am not of the world" (John 17:14).

What *does* the Christian have? Beyond the scorn of the world —bitter recompense for bearing fruit—what does the Christian receive for bearing spiritual love? The answer lies in Jesus' rich affirmation of the third prophetic principle: the Christian's reward lies in a safe haven, a sense of conviction and surety, and above all the experience of Christian joy.

This principle is threaded through all that Jesus says in these chapters in John. Jesus is no philosophical idealist. More than anyone, he is the psychological realist. He is the God who knows humanity by having made humanity *and* by being human. No other maker can make this claim. The artist may know his painting by having painted it, but he is not the painting itself. As God-become-human, Jesus knows the need of humanity for a haven, for security.

Jesus opens his discourse with a word of assurance to his disciples. Ahead of him lies his own agonizing torment in Gethsemane, and the dark path to Golgotha. Despite this, he says in words of inexpressible love, "Let not your hearts be troubled; believe in God, believe also in me" (John 14:1). The fact of the matter is that Jesus also sees beyond Gethsemane, beyond Golgotha, to the resurrection. On the basis of that he promises a resting place that is peace: "I go to prepare a place for you."

The first assurance lies in the promised haven in the life everlasting, but a second assurance applies to our daily Christian walk. To convict and assure us *now,* Jesus says that he "will pray the Father, and he will give you another Counselor, to be with you for ever" (John 14:16). The Greek word for "counselor" here can also be translated as "comforter," the "Spirit of truth" that dwells in us. In this spirit, Jesus says, he will be with us always: "I will not leave you desolate."

The Holy Spirit may be seen as the weld that unites us in the bond to Jesus and the Father, the fiery seal that binds our bridge indissolubly in spiritual union. But the Holy Spirit also provides two great rewards for those united in spiritual love: peace and joy. These comforting words of Jesus rise above the clash of swords and the darkness at Golgotha: "Peace I leave with you; my peace I give to you; not as the world gives do I give to you. Let not your hearts be troubled, neither let them be afraid" (John 14:27). Upon his friends Jesus bestows the unspeakable gift of peace; but, further, he promises joy. The very purpose of our abiding in Jesus' love is joy: "These things I have spoken to you, that my joy may be in you, and that your joy may be full" (John 15:11). Instead of gloom and agony in his waning hours, Jesus brings a message of joy—not a partial joy that eases the sorrow somewhat, but a joy that is full, that washes out sorrow. Several times in the ensuing verses, Jesus emphasizes the great promise: because we love Jesus, the Father loves us. Because of such love, our joy will be full.

Here on the eve of his captivity, Jesus speaks words of incomparable solace to his disciples. They are words above all of love, for the road ahead of him can only be walked out of love. In Jesus the Old Testament prophetic utterances and the dramatic reality of spiritual love meet in a power that shakes the foundations of the world. This love set the world on fire as it blazed in the hearts of the early believers. It didn't end there in the upper room. Later New Testament writers seized this theme and gave it dramatic intensity as they gave further instructions for nurturing the spiritual fruit of love.

For Discussion

In his book *The Four Loves,* C. S. Lewis distinguishes these four loves as (1) *affection,* which is perhaps the most common love; (2) *friendship,* which is a special bonding between people; (3) *eros,* which is romantic love, the "being in love" between a man and a woman; and (4) *charity* or *agape,* which is spiritual love, man's special relationship with God. If we have charity, how does that affect all our other kinds of love? The great biblical passage on love in 1 Corinthians 13 sheds light on the question. Are the other kinds of love gifts from God for our relationships with others?

We might also turn the question around. How is our love for a husband or wife like our love for God? How is our love for a friend like our love for God?

CHAPTER SEVEN

LOVE
Nurturing Love

"Got yo'sef a nice plot heah," he said. He squinted with sharp blue eyes through a face as seamed and lined as the southern Ohio hill soil I was working. His large hands were the color of old shoe leather, worn and wrinkled with long labor.

"Yep," he said, "jes needs somepin special."

I paused in my digging. Yes, I was proud of that garden, my first, which I had worked out of the heavy, red clay soil. I had worked compost into the soil and each spadeful now turned quick and easy. But it was good to stop and share ideas with the old-timer, my neighbor, a former coal miner and longtime gardener from down the dirt road a piece. He walked over often to tell me hill country lore—such things as how squirrel meat had it all beat over rabbit, if only it were easier to skin out.

"What yo' need," he was saying, "is some catfish makings. Tell yo' what. Me and the missus are fishing the river tonight for catfish. I'll bring over a bucket of scraps in the morning. Yo' work them in the soil aroun' the tomaters and yo'll see some tomaters!"

True to his word, he hailed me the next morning and had a large wash bucket full of fish scraps—stringy intestines, glassy-eyed heads—waiting for me. And true to his word, those "tomaters" produced like no tomatoes I had grown before or since. From two dozen unstaked plants, I literally had bushels of tomatoes. I stopped people on the road, handing out grocery bags full of ripe fruit that summer.

Part of the fun of gardening is sharing proven, successful tips. They form a kind of bond among gardeners. From one old-timer I learned where to plant marigolds—"Skeers off the bugs," he said. From another I learned where to plant onions, even though I don't like them. I learned how to compost around tomatoes, how to hill strawberries, how to stagger bean crops, how to interplant radishes. Each green space in my garden is a testimony to the advice of others. And the garden is its own reward.

Recognizing the central and absolute authority in the teachings of Jesus, we can also learn much about the practical nature of nurturing the spiritual fruit of love from writers in the New Testament. All of their teachings emanate from the central focus of Jesus' love, and his teachings are the groundwork for the practical suggestions.

To list all the evidence is nearly impossible, since, as a record of the origins of the Christian church, the New Testament epistles are brimful of teachings on love in the model of Jesus. Basically, however, two large directions are distinguished: love for the world and love for God.

The former, love for the world, is a perverted kind of love that ultimately folds inward on itself. Like the black hole in space, love of the world collapses in on itself. Such love is really *desire,* a weed in the garden of spiritual fruit that breeds wildly into covetousness, envy, and other such offspring.

In *The Great Divorce,* C. S. Lewis writes about the contrast between love for the world and love for God. He describes travelers who are transported from a greasy, gray town (the gray before either eternal night or eternal morning) to the outskirts of heaven. En route the travelers are compelled to make a choice about what they will love. Will they choose to be *in* love, in God's love, or will they insist upon loving themselves and the things of the world as they know it.

The particular insidiousness of love for the world is that people with this sort of love really, truly believe that they are the most important thing in the world. This, after all, is the world's message. Get before you're taken! Be number one! The world is yours for the taking! And so a number of the pale, ghostly voyagers on Lewis's pilgrimage believe. They always insist on *human rights,* on having things their own way. How tempting it is—to want to have things our way. When told to "ask for the

Bleeding Charity," one of Lewis's travelers responds, "I don't want charity. I'm a decent man and if I had my rights I'd have been here long ago and you can tell them I said so." No, love can't be done like that. At least not if we believe what Paul tells us in Ephesians 2:8-9: "For by grace you have been saved through faith; and this is not your own doing, it is the gift of God—not because of works, lest any man should boast." The message is not isolated to Ephesians; it is the central thread of the New Testament and particularly of Paul's teaching (see Rom. 3:23-24; 1 Cor. 1:30; Col. 1:14).

In contrast to those who love the world are those who walk in the love of God. One cannot pursue both sorts of love. This is the great either/or of the New Testament. In his first epistle, John makes it clear: "Do not love the world or the things in the world. If any one loves the world, love for the Father is not in him" (1 John 2:15). John points out that love for the world is always transient, passing away like a wind on a summer day, but love for God is eternal, and "he who does the will of God abides for ever" (1 John 2:17).

That word *abide* is an important one for John. He uses it repeatedly in describing the active, ongoing Christian walk with God. To abide does not mean to do nothing. The word does suggest rest and peace, and rightfully so. But it is an active verb, a kind of doing. It may best be understood as walking hand-in-hand, inseparably, with God. David C. Needham has explained this abiding in God, and the Spirit abiding in us, with the analogy of a woman pregnant with child. One can rightfully say that the child is in the mother and the mother in the child. We may extend Needham's analogy here by also saying that what the mother does, so the unborn child does. If one abides in God's love, one will do what God does.

What typifies such love? Consider these qualities as a beginning point. Love that abides in God is *not* afraid. It is unusual to answer a question by saying what the thing is not, but it is important to our Christian understanding of the spiritual fruit of love to do so in this case. John writes: "There is no fear in love, but perfect love casts out fear" (1 John 4:18). Love for the world is often fearful. People with this sort of love fear that they aren't getting what they *deserve*. Believers in Christian love have already received far more than they ever deserved—life eternal. This in itself casts out fear. When we add the concept that we now *abide* in Jesus, to whom has been given all authority under heaven and earth, we can be courageous in our acts of love.

How, then, do we exercise the courage of love? Our first responsibility, as John suggests in his epistle, is to strengthen our own assurance and the assurance of others by proclaiming the gospel. According to John, this loving act affirms our own faith as well. He stipulates three specific aspects to proclamation. First, we "testify that the Father has sent his Son as the Savior of the world" (1 John 4:14). This is the startling good news of redemption, the love of God incarnate. Second, we make salvation real and vital in our personal, spoken testimony. And, third, we "know and believe the love God has for us." We strengthen our own faith for active engagement of the world. We do not set our Christian life on a back shelf; we bring it to the world.

How do we bring our love to the world? The answer lies in the example of Jesus and the testimony of the entire New Testament. We offer our love in servanthood. Those who have love for the world ultimately love themselves; those who have love for God ultimately love God's creation. This servanthood extends to stewardship over all God's creation—we will treat the birds of the air and the air itself, the beasts of the field and the field itself, the fish of the sea and the sea itself in love. Surely God created the world good; he has said so. Just as surely humanity has blighted and scarred this perfectly created world. Christians have the urgent task of redeeming that creation in love. In short, Christians must exercise a care for the global ecology motivated by love for God, not love for the things of this world. That may well mean that we will have to do without some of the things of this world in order to preserve God's creation.

Above all, however, we must exercise the servanthood of love toward our fellow humans, whom we believe can also be redeemed by the power and authority of Jesus' love. Here, more than ever, we must conceive of love as *active*. Instead of waiting for others to come to us, we must reach out to others. In what ways? Jesus answers clearly: "Then they also will answer, 'Lord, when did we see thee hungry or thirsty or a stranger or naked or sick or in prison, and did not minister to thee?' Then he will answer them, 'Truly, I say to you, as you did it not to one of the least of these, you did it not to me'" (Matt. 25:44-45).

Servanthood, furthermore, will require us to take firm and active stands on the great moral issues of our age. For example, love refuses to accept abortion as legitimate, for it transgresses both the law of God and the law of love. Not only must we act against that evil, but we must also act to bring solace to children born out of wedlock and to their mothers. The law of God and the law of love require us to act against infanticide: "Rescue those who are being taken away to death; hold back those who are stumbling to the slaughter. If you say, 'Behold, we did not know this,' does not he who weighs the heart perceive it? Does not he who keeps watch over your soul know it, and will he not requite man according to his work?" (Prov. 24:11-12). The law of God and the law of love require us to honor life, to be God's agents and servants in its preservation and redemption.

The fruit of love grows from the True Vine, the central stalk of Jesus in our lives. If the vine withers there, all our spiritual fruit is jeopardized. Those who cannot love will not have joy or peace or patience. Love makes these fruits possible—God's eternal, sacrificial love for us and our abiding in his love, proclaiming his message, casting out fear, caring for his creation, working as servants in the vineyard of his kingdom.

For Discussion

Jesus was born in the lineage of David—the fulfillment of the earthly kingship as the King of kings. David was God's chosen, earthly king as Jesus was God's chosen King of kings. Both David and Jesus had friendships that were important to them.

Friendship remains an important kind of love for the Christian. What can we learn about our friendship-love by considering that of David with Jonathan?

How important were Jesus' friendships to him? You might consider the trial at Gethsemane, recorded in Luke 22:39-53. Here Jesus also experienced the pain that sometimes accompanies friendship. We all might have times when friendship hurts; at such times we do well to remember the words of Proverbs 18:24, "there is a friend who sticks closer than a brother."

CHAPTER EIGHT

JOY
A God Who Laughs

Once a group of Buddhist scholars considered the weighty question of whether the Buddha, that figure of supreme serenity and harmony and dispassion, ever laughed. In careful scrutiny of their holy books, they concluded that indeed the Buddha may have smiled upon at least one occasion. In fact, to establish their case they borrowed an early work on Indian theater that distinguished six kinds of laughter, ranging from the refined, slight smile of the spiritual leader to the raucous laughter of common people. Almost as if laughter were profane!

The peculiar wonder of Christianity is that Christians have a Savior who wants joy! Jesus is so in touch with our common, human condition—having walked with his people and, beyond question, having laughed with them—that he desires nothing more than that our joy be made full. It is a rare and wonderful thing among the many religions of the world that Christianity cherishes humor, laughter, and joy.

Christians seldom take note of the humor of Jesus in their Christianity, or indeed of the rich role given to humor throughout Scripture. This is understandable, for at the very heart of Christianity is Christ on the cross, an event of such great solemnity, when our sins were redeemed by the death of the Son of God, that we approach our faith with awe, reverence, and worship. Jesus is the one foreseen as the "man of sorrows and acquainted with grief," the one whose path in life leads resolutely to Golgotha, the place of the Skull, the place of death. And yet to be one acquainted with grief is not necessarily to be one overwhelmed by grief, to be one who is disheartened and discouraged. Nothing at all in Jesus' life testifies to that. Indeed, the glory of the Savior is that, although a man of sorrows and acquainted with grief, he is also the one who has promised us and provided us with joy unspeakable and full of glory. His life is witness to joyous living, not the down-turned head and tear-stained cheek but the head lifted to receive blessing and honor and glory. His vision is that of Isaiah and John: every tear shall be wiped from their cheek by the hand of God. We forget that beyond Golgotha lies the empty grave and the resurrection. We forget that the gospel is not the bad news of a death but the good news of spiritual wholeness. The ministry of Jesus, if anything, is to such wholeness. In *The Humor of Christ* (New York: Harper & Row, 1975), Elton Trueblood writes that "We do not know with certainty how much humor there is in Christ's teachings, but we can be sure there is far more than is normally recognized."

Why don't we seize the humor of Jesus, the joy of the gospel? Why do we so often sing hymns in worship services as if we have a pinched nerve or acid indigestion? Henry David Thoreau wrote in *Walden* that "There is nowhere recorded a simple and irrepressible satisfaction with the gift of life, any memorable praise of God." To achieve that memorable praise we do well to ask what are the biblical patterns for humor and then, specifically, what of the humor of Jesus?

Surprisingly, it begins in the Old Testament, which fairly crackles with laughter. There are individual moments such as when David returned with the ark of the covenant to Jerusalem and danced along with the people in an ecstasy of good cheer. Michal must have been a kind of dour woman, or at least a bit jealous, for she rebuked David with savage irony: "Michal the daughter of Saul came out to meet David, and said, 'How the king of Israel honored himself today, uncovering himself today before the eyes of his servants' maids, as one of the vulgar fellows shamelessly uncovers himself!'" (2 Sam. 6:20). But David refused to let his joy diminish under her mockery: "And David said to Michal, 'It was before the Lord, who chose me above your father, and above all his house, to appoint me as prince over Israel, the people of the Lord—and I will make merry before the Lord. I will make myself yet more contemptible than this, and I will be abased in your eyes; but by the maids of whom you have spoken, by them I shall be held in honor.'" Here we have a familiar biblical pattern—one dares make himself contemptible before men in his joy in the Lord. Indeed, and without question, David serves in this passage as a type of Jesus, who, as fulfillment, also made himself contemptible on the cross before the proud and noble of his time so that our joy may be full.

How can one cite all the examples of humor in the Old Testament? Let me offer just a few examples.

1. *Moses and Pharoah.* Moses was an unlikely leader, with a temper so hot that he killed a man; he was doing penance in the desert when the Lord called on him. And even after the Lord performed miracles for him, Moses was still trying to talk his way out of it. "I'm not eloquent," he said as he argued fiercely. "Who made man's mouth?" responded the Lord. And the performance of the miracles themselves in Egypt provided a kind of comic routine. The Lord at first allowed miracles that the Egyptian magicians could match with their sorcery, almost as if he were teasing them. But God allowed them only enough power to show them how puny it really was; in the end he stretched forth his almighty arm in authority beyond their comprehension. In effect, the Lord made fools of the magicians. It would have been better for them if they had never tried. Then they could have said, "We could have done that too." God demonstrated indisputably what they could not do.

2. *Elijah and the Prophets of Baal.* A second scenario, again based upon almighty power and authority against human claims to power, occurred in Elijah's taunting of the prophets of Baal. This is one of the few instances of overt mockery in the Bible, and we note it here for later reference. Only seldom does mockery, used by God's agents, appear in Scripture, and then it is directed at the most mighty and diabolical of God's opponents. Those who deck themselves in the apparel of pride will be made fools before God. Only the proud and antagonistic are mocked, and then by a God who says he will not be mocked. So it is that we can imagine the inward humor Elijah felt as he attacked the paragons of pride: "And at noon Elijah mocked them, saying, 'Cry aloud, for he is a god; either he is musing, or he has gone aside, or he is on a journey, or perhaps he is asleep and must be

awakened'" (1 Kings 18:27). And we remember how the fire of the Lord came down to consume Elijah's offering.

3. *Belshazzar.* A third instance comes to mind, this in the rule of Belshazzar, last of the Babylonian kings in the time of Daniel, around 540 B.C. At Belshazzar's own feast to celebrate his power, he used the sacred vessels of gold and silver that Nebuchadnezzar had taken from the sacred temple, and with these he served wine and toasted the gods of gold and silver. In effect, Belshazzar was mocking the Lord in a fit of proud debauchery. We note in Daniel 5:5 that "immediately the fingers of a man's hand appeared and wrote on the plaster of the wall." And also immediately, at this astonishing sight, the king's limbs gave way and his knees knocked together. Again, the proud man was made the ridiculous clown, the fool, before God's power.

We see a pattern of humor and comic derision in the Old Testament, the good humor of a heart overflowing with joy, and a comic derision following upon the revelation of God's almighty power which reveals the proud man as a fool. But what of the New Testament, and particularly of the Lord Immanuel, the God with us, Jesus?

It is fruitful to note first what kind of humor Jesus does not use. He does not use mockery, for mockery is always demeaning. We noted that Elijah mocked the proud and desperate of Baal, demeaning them before God's power. But Elijah is not the Son of God. Only once does Jesus come close to mockery, and again it is against the haughtiest, proudest, most insufferable people of his age, the Pharisees and Sadducees. "Woe to you, you whitened sepulchres!" Jesus says. But even here, Jesus' anger overrides mockery in a kind of subtle irony. Anger? Jesus is irate with these loveless legalists, to be sure. He does prophesy woe to these pompous autocrats of the law. But irony more closely typifies Jesus' humor. The Pharisees and Sadducees were trivialists; everything was ordered for them, including their white stone temples. Jesus refers ironically to the leaders in these white temples as whitened sepulchres because they had buried love beneath the burden of legalism.

We should note, furthermore, that Jesus himself was routinely mocked until the very moment of his death (Matt. 27:41-43). The crowd mocked him by crowning him with thorns, by spit-

ting on him, by scourging him, by jeering at him, by placing a
sign above his head on the cross reading "Jesus of Nazareth:
King of the Jews!" The mean spirit of mockery was directed at
Jesus, not from him.

We note, then, that Jesus does not use mockery. Nor does he
indulge in the sort of dark, grim, macabre humor that is so
prevalent today. We live in an age of the so-called "sick joke."
Jesus was a healer and would have no patience for the sick joke
which grovels in people's infirmity.

Put positively, Jesus' humor is characterized by two counterparts to mockery and dark humor. First, in opposition to mockery, Jesus' humor is always characterized by love. His humor
builds up. Even though he is the Son of God, he has reached
down to humans to lift them up. He understands humankind
completely, for he has given life. Here the promises of the New
Testament take on new bearing, as in John 15:11: "These things
I have spoken to you, that my joy may be in you, and that your
joy may be full." Second, in opposition to dark humor, Jesus'
humor illumines. It shows us a new hope—the hope of what we
can be as redeemed children of God. It shows us a new way, the
way of the resurrection and life everlasting.

What, then, are the practical, concrete examples of Jesus'
humor? At the risk of overlap, I like to classify such examples
into the following categories, which, it seems to me, demonstrate
the broad, rich range of Jesus' humor.

First, riddles have been a key component of humor for ages.
Samson riddled in the Old Testament, which indicates an appre-
ciation for this peculiarly gentle kind of wit in ancient times.
Jesus demonstrates a special fondness for the riddle. To the
Jews he says, "Destroy this temple, and in three days I will raise it
up" (John 2:19). How? It took forty years to build that temple.
John gives us the answer to the riddle: it discloses the meaning
of Jesus' divine nature. The sacred temple of his own body will
be destroyed, but he will arise from death in three days. Jesus
puts a riddle to Nicodemus: "Unless one is born anew, he cannot
see the kingdom of God." Nicodemus doesn't perceive the riddle. "How can a man be born when he is old?" he retorts, one
imagines with some disgust. "Can he enter a second time into his
mother's womb and be born?" (John 3:3-4). Again, the answer to

the riddle lies in Jesus, in whom all who believe are born anew. And a third time, when the disciples ask Jesus to eat, he offers a riddle: "I have food to eat of which you do not know." The disciples put their befuddled heads together, "Has any one brought him food?" Jesus responds that "My food is to do the will of him who sent me, and to accomplish his work" (John 4:31-34). We still partake of that food—in the sacrament surely, but also as we do his divine will. This is spiritual nourishment. The answer lies in Jesus himself, in whom all our spiritual riddles end.

A second category of Jesus' humor is the witty remark, the quick response which reveals an adroit mind rooted in good humor. Again, each of these responses, through their gentle and loving humor, also provides a spiritual lesson. We might say that of course Jesus always has the right answer. But it is amazing and amusing how often his right answer is witty, turning the listeners inward on their own spiritual need.

A third kind of humor shows Jesus simply enjoying the rich interchange of human fellowship. One such example occurs at the wedding feast in Cana. He did not have to change the water into wine. Clearly, it demonstrates his power, but it is not an overt act against evil such as the healing of a paralytic or the cleansing of the Gadarene demoniac. Rather, it is for the good humor of his beloved companions. Best of all, Jesus changes the water into the best wine of the evening. Only a God with a sense of humor and a desire for human well-being would do this. Such humor is situational, arising from normal human conditions, and has as its end simple human joy.

And yet a fourth kind of humor typifies Jesus: irony. In irony there is always a gap between expectations and result, between intention and implication, between knowledge and ignorance. Into that gap humor enters.

Jesus usually uses irony with opponents, those locked in ignorance, and seldom with his familiar friends. The irony is meant to pique these opponents, to nudge them toward seeking the true thing being suggested or disclosed. We find such an instance in Mark 12 when Jesus gives his well-known "render to Caesar" response. The irony, of course, lies in the fact that his questioners have not rendered to God the things due to him.

Above all, however, I find simple joy, simple lovingkindness and good will toward men typifying Jesus' humor. For humor is also a way of looking at life, a way of capturing the big picture, of seeing small details in the light of divine grace. He poses a riddle to the Samaritan woman at the well in order to lead her to the joy of living water. Jesus wishes health for his children. In his book *The Humor of Jesus* (New York: Alba House, 1977), Henri Cormier points out that Jesus never invites the sick to go to bed. He never told anyone to lie down on the analyst's couch. If someone is in bed, even on a deathbed, he tells them to get up. Often he offers his hand to help them. While we will suffer anguish in our walk through a fallen life, as we noted in Chapter Four, we are comforted in our Christian living to know that God wishes us health.

There is also often a playfulness in Jesus' humor. He names two of his disciples, James and John, the Sons of Thunder. He shows his quick wit when he calls Peter, the fisherman, a fisher of men.

As Cormier points out, Jesus' humor "dispells darkness from our hearts." Cormier gives the example of the woman caught in adultery. While the law-bringers charged her, Jesus wrote in the dirt with his finger. At last the expected trap was sprung. "What do you say about it?" they asked Jesus. You know his answer to the Pharisees: "Let him who is without sin among you be the first to throw a stone at her." Jesus doesn't condemn; he converts. He doesn't tie us in darkness; he frees us to light and deliverance.

One of the wonders and joys of Christianity is that we do indeed have a God who laughs. Our God is not remote or distant. In fact, Jesus' humor is always opposed to arrogance, against any separation of person from person. If Jesus is surely one "acquainted with grief," he is just as surely one acquainted with laughter who wishes for his children nothing less than joy.

For Discussion

The Bible literally bursts with joy. Can you think of other examples of joyous expression in the Old Testament? In the life of

Jesus? What does it mean to us personally to know we have a God who laughs?

Perhaps the greatest source of joy to the Christian lies in the fact that this world is not our final home. This life is not the end of things. The New Testament closes in a picture of the most remarkable joy for the Christian, the new heaven and earth of our eternal home. What are some of the traits of that eternal home? You might consider passages such as Revelation 5:9-14; 7:13-17; and 21:1-8.

CHAPTER NINE

JOY
Steps on the Way to Joy

The third-grade teacher was getting to know her students on that first day of school, asking a question to elicit their inner feelings. The question was "What makes you happy?" Every teacher, I would guess, wants happy pupils. Who wants to live eight hours of the day with long faces?

She might have anticipated the responses of her third-grade charges. "I want a computer. A computer would make me happy," said one. Another responded, "Barbie and Ken dolls make me happy." A third, "Recess makes me happy."

We might anticipate that from third graders—things and events make them happy. In a sense, adults also tend to measure their happiness by things and events. This is not altogether bad or unusual. A quiet home to relax in may make us happy. A family camping trip may make us happy. Yet, there is a kind of happiness that is more than simply "being happy"—and that is joy. Is joy just something longed for, something we see faint glimmers of in this life, like the sun spraying its splendor from behind a cloud only to be shut off by the next wind? Is joy something we reach for but can't quite touch, perhaps something like the wind itself? It seems that everyone yearns for joy that will endure beyond the moment's happiness, joy that undergirds even sorrow. This yearning is not just for something that happens while living, but rather for a way of living.

The meaning of the word *gospel* is "good news." And the good news is that there is such a joy, a joy that endures beyond happiness, a joy that is present even in sorrow. That is joy inexpressible and full of glory. And the good word of the good news is that the Bible teaches the way of joy. Scripture tells us both the *way* to joy and the *nature* of true joy as a quality of life rooted in God rather than as a passing emotion.

To be sure, we rightly associate joy with being happy. A person who bears the fruit of joy can hardly help being happy. But it is not necessarily true that by being happy we have the fruit of joy. Why is this? All too often we equate our happiness with things that make us happy: a new car, a pay raise, a lovely and comfortable house. The glory of joy is that we can bear this fruit without such means, since joy is never allied with things of this world. Thus, the author of Hebrews says, "You had compassion on the prisoners, and you joyfully accepted the plundering of your property, since you knew that you yourselves had a better possession and an abiding one" (Heb. 10:34). The passage clearly indicates not only that possessions are *not* to be considered the means to joy but that we can be joyful even when our possessions are plundered.

If the first step to the spiritual fruit of joy is recognition that it does not reside in the material possessions of this world, then the second step is recognition that the way to joy begins in obedience to God. The writer of Chronicles says, "Let the hearts of those who seek the Lord rejoice" (1 Chron. 16:10). Obedience gives the surety that sets the heart at ease. This is the prepared ground, the fertile soil from which joy can spring up into full fruit.

Perhaps no other theme is so common as this in the psalms of King David. The joy he testifies to in these great songs of comfort was hewn out of a rough and rocky life; indeed, David often seems to have been most obedient in hardship. When persecuted and pursued by Saul, holed up in ragged desert bluffs, hungry and accompanied by only a few hundred faithful men, David testified to his joy rooted in obedience to God. The desert is unfertile ground for happiness, but as a place of testing it gave rise to joy for David. "Let all who take refuge in thee rejoice," he wrote; "let them ever sing for joy." In the familiar Psalm 19, David gives specific testimony to the way of obedience as the way to joy. In verses 7-10 he celebrates six points of the law and commandments of God, declaring that each is a way of increasing human joy and wisdom. He was tried in the desert and led to joy; but David was also a trial, one who too readily and too easily transgressed the law of the Lord. Each time he learned that he had to get back on the way of obedience to get to joy. David provided a living testament to the words of Nehemiah: "The joy of the Lord is your strength" (Neh. 8:10).

If joy is not to be associated with material possessions that may, nonetheless, make us happy, and if the way to joy begins in the way of obedience to God, then the third step to joy in the Christian life is understanding that joy is a blessing of God through the operation of the Holy Spirit. There is always a fine line between the gifts of the Holy Spirit—the charismatic gifts, which include, for example, the gifts of hospitality or of healing—and the fruit of the spirit that we consider here. Both are discovered through a close walk with God, but the fruits, unlike the individualized special gifts God has given to spread his word and build his church, are available to all Christians in their Christian walk. We nurture and consciously develop the fruits of the spirit and yet we also recognize that they are blessings upon our Christian life. We might say that though we nurture the fruit on our human spiritual ground, God rewards our attempts by sending the rich rain of his Spirit to make the fruit flourish. This is a glorious truth; we are never left alone to develop our fruit. God wants us to do so, and he sends the encouragement of his Spirit to assist us. Note that when the disciples worked to do God's will, they "were filled with joy and with the Holy Spirit" (Acts 13:52).

The fourth, and perhaps most important, step on the way to joy is understanding that we can possess true joy even in the presence of sorrow. In Isaiah 55, the prophet tells us that those who repent are to be blessed, that they are to seek the Lord, that God's word is sure, and that on the basis of that word "you shall go out in joy, and be led forth in peace" (Isa. 55:12). Mourning shall turn to dancing. In the Gospel of Luke, the physician tells us that the angel announced to the shepherds, "I bring you good news of a great joy which will come to all people; for to you is born this day in the city of David a Savior, who is Christ the Lord" (Luke 2:10-11). That which turns our mourning steps into the flight of dancing is Jesus. But what does this mean in the New Testament? On an evening before his own death, while he foresaw and awaited the agony of Calvary, Jesus said to his disciples, "These things I have spoken to you, that my joy may be in you, and that your joy may be full" (John 15:11). Surely, Jesus also foresaw the suffering that awaited the disciples as they proclaimed his word: death, punishment, torture, imprisonment. That your joy may be full!

This makes no sense to the secular world, yet it is a truth attested to over and over in the New Testament. If the theme of the New Testament is the "good news," it is also joy—joy that overcomes mourning. The good news of the New Testament is, in fact, precisely this: that joy can endure and arise even in sorrow.

From his imprisonment Paul wrote to the church at Colossae, "Now I rejoice in my sufferings" (Col. 1:24). Peter, who talks about the "fiery ordeal" of Christian suffering, encourages believers to "rejoice in so far as you share Christ's sufferings, that you may also rejoice and be glad when his glory is revealed" (1 Pet. 4:13). And James, that practical and purposeful apostle, tells us to "count it all joy, my brethren, when you meet various trials" (James 1:2).

Who among us hasn't undergone trial? Indeed, for some of us it sometimes seems that joy has fled behind a gray cloud. At times like that I think of a canoe trip I once took with my family.

I have canoed on many rivers. There is something about the silver dip and feather of oars on the face of the river that frees the human spirit. And each river has its own personality. In northern Pennsylvania the powerful Clarion laughs at the canoer, tricks him with a hundred secret whirlpools and eddies. In Michigan, the Au Sable threads through pine so silent and still that the canoer holds his breath while paddling. But Michigan's White River in autumn after a hard rain is the unforgettable one. The banks are littered with massive torn trunks full of earth and fury. The sky is gray and lowering, and strange figures rampage in the forest mists. Great trunks arch over the river, submerged logs rise to strike at the canoe. It is a dark river, and it seems like a ride through death, cold and wet and clammy. The White River bears the whiteness of cerement cloth.

I canoed this river with my family when the children were

young; my wife in the prow, the children arranged youngest to oldest, each with a lifejacket, I in the back as steersman. We left on the dawn of a cheerless and gloomy day, the water a dark brown, the sky as gray and vapor-laden as a grave. And from the back I could watch the muscles tense on their young backs, could see the sudden shock of fear on their faces as a trunk toppled in the forest and fell sodden to the earth, could hear their words— "Something moved there. Is it a ghost?"

I rode the river praying for light.

There is this about the river: there is no getting off until you reach the end. Once committed, you stay the cold and dangerous course until you reach the end, using every skill, every trick you know to hold that fragile vessel upright through every grim thing that rises to confront you.

We made twenty miles by noon, and beached the canoe at the first shallow we found, a small spit of shore that angled out from a high bluff. We found a course up the bluff to eat our lunch on its crest. Looking down on the dark trail of the river, we shivered and sat close together and ate silently.

Then, with a sudden slap at the gray clouds, the sun broke through. Wet leaves flashed with crimson splendor. Birds we hadn't heard all morning suddenly careened through the air, calling and quarreling in the golden light. We lay back on the blankets and laughed and pretended our hearts weren't pounding.

It was the same river in the afternoon, but a river full of light and laughter. So too in the Christian life, we often find ourselves on a journey seeking the blessed release of joy.

Jesus never called us to the "good life" as measured by today's standards. He didn't promise us "quality of life" in the words of today's language. He didn't even promise we'd always be happy. He called us to a life of servanthood, and his promise is joy. But because this joy is fixed in the eternal word of our Lord, it is sure even when our good life turns bad, when we disqualify for quality of life, when our happiness is overwhelmed with sorrow. The joy of the Lord which is our strength lies in the perfect peace he provides, the same peace he promised his disciples when he appeared to that poor, bewildered, frightened group and said,

"Why are you troubled, and why do questionings rise in your hearts?" (Luke 24:38). Here we see that in Jesus the words of Isaiah are fulfilled: "Thou dost keep him in perfect peace, whose mind is stayed on thee" (Isa. 26:3). The Hebrew term for "perfect peace" is roughly equivalent to a mathematical formula: peace times peace, peace squared. It is the unimaginable peace of the heart that leans on Jesus for its joy.

A distinction between the good life and joy? Between quality of life and joy? Between happiness and joy? Paul makes it clear in his letter to the Romans: "For the kingdom of God is not food and drink but righteousness and peace and joy in the Holy Spirit" (Rom. 14:17). The three go together like a perfect triangle: righteousness—our servanthood in Jesus' name; joy—the fruit that grows from righteousness; and peace—Jesus' gracious provision for those who endure even in adversity.

When Jesus taught the people, little children—not nicely dressed and freshly bathed, but children of the village with skinned knees and dirty noses—gathered around him. The disciples wanted to shoo them away. But Jesus called them to him, dirty noses and all, and declared them examples of what we must be like to enter the kingdom of heaven. For Jesus, the least of these count.

As we seek to do Jesus' will in this world, we remind ourselves of that fact—that each of us is a little one, the least of these. Each of us is fallen and abides in a fallen world. Who among us, at some time or even most of the time, has not suffered from loneliness? While all the others seem to soar on wings of eagles, we seem to limp on sore feet. Who among us hasn't had to make lonely and anguishing decisions? Some of us may have battled the black cloud of depression, perhaps learning that God's way is in that sea also, but that it is still so very hard to battle the waves. Who among us, at some time or even most of the time, hasn't suffered the anguish of illness, if not of ourselves then of someone whom we love very much? Who among us hasn't had our feelings hurt, or hurt the feelings of others and wished we hadn't? Herein lies our common "leastness." We are imperfect people groping our way to a light we feel is there but don't always see clearly.

But, although fallen and living in a fallen world, we are God's children. Even though we have wounded the good that he created, his goodness is absolute and abides to heal all our wounds. All of us who call ourselves by his name also abide in his will. There we learn that although we limp on sore feet, he will strengthen the weak knees that kneel before him. There we learn that although we founder in the sea, his way is in the sea, that he still controls the waves and says "Peace, be still." There we learn that although we battle illness and death in this brief journey through life, we have his promise that he will wipe away every tear from our eyes. Where is *there?* It is safe in the arms of Jesus, the same arms to which he called, and still calls, the little children, the least of these.

For Discussion

In many motel and hotel rooms around the world, the Gideons have placed copies of the Bible. Many of these editions list an index of verses of special comfort or praise. Are there passages of the Bible you have particularly treasured? How have they acquired personal relevance at different times of your life?

One of the joys of Christian life is to know we have a biblical, divinely authorized mandate for living, that the Bible can give us clear guidance on pertinent, daily issues of life. Our joy lies in the confidence that we are doing the right thing according to God's Word. This dispels confusion and doubt, two enemies of joy.

For example, today there is much debate on issues of life such as abortion, infanticide, and euthanasia. What does the Bible have to say about these? You might consider the answers in such passages as Deuteronomy 30:19; 1 Samuel 16:7; Psalms 127:3 and 139:13-16; Proverbs 6:16-17 and 24:11-12; Ecclesiastes 11:5; Isaiah 44:24; Jeremiah 1:5; Matthew 18:10, 14 and 25:44-45; and Galatians 1:15-16.

When discussing such issues, however, we can also see the dynamics of the fruits of the spirit coming to bear upon them.

Are we bringing to the issues the fruit of love, for example? Too often it is easy to be judgmental and vindictive. In an essay collected in *The Zero People* (Ann Arbor: Servant Books, 1983), John Powell, S.J., professor of theology at Loyola University, strikes the better course when he pleads,

> Let's be sure to speak up out of love, however, not out of judgment or hatred toward those who perform or who have had abortions. I have been involved with a lot of prolife work, and I'm convinced that one thing that could short-circuit this whole movement would be for it to become infected with vindictiveness or hate. If we want to stand up for the sacredness of human life, we have to speak up out of love—love for the babies who won't see life, and for the frightened women who often don't understand what they're going through, and even for the abortionists who somehow believe that the killing is necessary. We can judge the action of abortion and say loudly and clearly that it is terribly wrong, but we should not take on ourselves God's role in judging the subjective responsibility of individuals. (Pp. 10-11)

The question we must ask is this: How does love motivate and direct my action?

CHAPTER TEN

JOY
Joy as Fellowship

In the preceding two chapters we noted first that Christians do indeed have a God who laughs, who understands and wants joy for us, and second that the way to human joy lies in obedience to our God. Now we turn to a third aspect of joy: fellowship among believers. Reflect for a few minutes on fellowship—our need for it, the biblical basis for it, what it is, and how we can develop it in the community of believers.

Why do we need fellowship? I believe there is a tremendous need in the church today for people to grow close together. Psychologists tell us that despite all the activities of our time that *throw* people together, we remain lonely. Perhaps that is because people are simply thrown together rather than drawn together. In our modern society, it is possible for a person to work an entire lifetime with others he or she has nothing in common with. They can be virtual strangers for eight to ten hours a day, punching in and punching out and in between complaining about how tired they are. Such a situation drives people to fill their loneliness in the quickest and most tragic ways.

This human need challenges the modern church to provide fellowship, for fellowship gives an enduring cure for loneliness and an enduring alternative to the cheap and quick rush of the contemporary idea that passes for joy. Fellowship provides quality of life rather than quantity of life. And herein also lies the compelling attraction of the church: when people experience its fellowship, they sense that they are worth something, that Jesus loves them for who they are and not for what they have done, and that they have a place among the believers.

What does the Bible have to say about meeting this need? We

find clear, undergirding principles for fellowship in Scripture, including, for example, the teaching of 1 Corinthians 12:4-27, which discusses our unity as one body, and John 13:3-20, which shows Jesus in fellowship with his disciples. A fascinating picture unfolds, however, in the story of Abraham recorded in Genesis 18:1-8.

It was a hot day, and Abraham was resting in the shade of his tent under the oak trees near Mamre. In the intense heat, things seemed to slide and shift before his eyes. But suddenly he started. Three men stood on the plain before his tent. Notice what actions Abraham took. First, "when he saw them, he ran from the tent door to meet them, and bowed himself to the earth." He then got up, went to them, and offered himself as a servant to their needs. Now, he didn't know these men. This was an act of reaching out, the first stage of fellowship. To have fellowship one must, first of all, get up, go out, and be a servant. Furthermore, Abraham saw to their comfort on this sweltering day: "Let a little water be brought, and wash your feet, and rest yourselves under the tree." Here we see a second important part of fellowship: one provides comfort for the stranger and invites that stranger in. And third, Abraham saw to their physical nourishment, urging them to rest "while I fetch a morsel of bread, that you may refresh yourselves." We remember that Jesus also spoke about offering "a cup of cold water in my name." Abraham does that. Fellowship nourishes. Though we may offer a cup of coffee rather than cold water, the principle is the same. Get up, go out, be a servant. See to their comfort and invite them in. Offer them something by way of refreshment. It seems fairly simple, doesn't it? But there's more to the story of Christian fellowship.

The word for fellowship in the Bible is *koinonia,* used sometimes as a noun, sometimes as a verb. In 2 Corinthians 13:14, for example, we read "the fellowship of the Holy Spirit be with you," and the Greek word for fellowship there is *koinonia.* But to understand this *koinonia* in the lives of believers, it is helpful to understand it in the light of a more common English word.

At the heart of fellowship is the idea of sharing something

held in common, and this sharing may be understood in three modern words, all of which derive from one Latin root word for "the things we hold in common." Consider first the word *community*. We live in a community, with other people. The church may provide community, for community is a physical thing. What do we hold in common as a church community? We share a common faith, a need for salvation, and a common spirit. The church provides a physical place for this community of believers to join together. Second, as a group of believers we surely might join in *communication*—again, a physical act of talking together about those things we hold in common and an important act, for without communication we cannot have the third aspect or spiritual sharing—*communion*. The Holy Spirit provides this communion, which is the closest of the three terms to denoting the biblical sense of fellowship. It is akin to the sacrament of the Lord's Supper, in which the physical elements lead us to a spiritual relationship. Fellowship, then, should be understood as something done by the Holy Spirit through people.

So we see both vertical and horizontal aspects of fellowship, aspects in which a living relationship with the Holy Spirit radiates outward to touch the lives of others. To define this relationship more closely, consider these qualifications. *Koinōnia* is not simply social fellowship. A community provides this. But fellowship is *by* the Spirit *through* people; the church can assist by providing structures for community. Furthermore, fellowship should not be understood as some mystic union with a transcendent being. It is given by the Spirit through people, but also for people. One might well ask whether this doesn't separate fellowship from the established church. To a certain degree it does, in the sense that fellowship does not *depend* upon the church. What then is the task of the church? To be sure, the church can encourage fellowship by providing communities, or structures, but this point bears repeating: fellowship cannot be consigned to organizations. It is something people *do*, in the power and authority of the Holy Spirit. The primary task of the church always has been and always will be the preaching of the Word. And, as someone once remarked to me, "There will be no fellowship in a church in which Christ is not preached." That is the tie between organization and individual; fellowship, however, must be understood as the task of the individual believer.

But why have fellowship? Why worry about it? Precisely because the joy that is ours as a fruit of the spirit must also nourish others. We don't nurture any of our fruits merely to please ourselves. Paul makes this perfectly clear: "Blessed be the God and Father of our Lord Jesus Christ, the Father of mercies and God of all comfort, who comforts us in all our affliction, so that we may be able to comfort those who are in any affliction, with the comfort with which we ourselves are comforted by God" (2 Cor. 1:3-4). Fellowship begins by reaching out to others to give them something they need—the joy we have so abundantly in Jesus.

What, then, might be some practical ways to exercise fellowship? Basically we should reach out to meet need wherever it is found, but there are some more specific and practical suggestions as well.

We should understand that fellowship begins in the home, with those with whom we have closest community, share the most in common, and communicate the most. An essential part of home fellowship is family devotions, which may range from daily readings to celebrations of special events.

Nearly a dozen years ago our family began using an advent wreath to celebrate the Christmas season, a pleasure that involves the whole family. One person lights the candles, another reads from an advent booklet geared to the youngest child, the children select songs to sing, and we have a circle prayer. After the brief time of spiritual fellowship in which everyone participates, eyes shining in the candlelight, the children blow out the candles. For a month before Christmas the advent wreath is a center for fellowship in the home.

A second practical dimension of fellowship is hospitality. But here one should distinguish between entertaining, which is inviting friends over with the expectation of being invited back eventually, and fellowship. Hospitality as fellowship is rooted in Luke 14:12-14, where Jesus gives his parable of the man at the marriage feast who says, "When you give a dinner or a banquet, do not invite your friends or your brothers or your kinsmen or your rich neighbors, lest they also invite you in return, and you be repaid." Hospitality doesn't invite people over with expectation of a return visit. Hospitality, as with Abraham, tells us to get up, go out, and provide for others so that they may share our joy. The parable tells us who these others are: "when you give a feast, invite the poor, the maimed, the lame, the blind, and you will be blessed, because they cannot repay you. You will be repaid at the resurrection of the just." Indeed, those who have a heart open to the joy of Jesus, those who nurture the fruit of joy, will also have an open home.

A third suggestion is to practice fellowship and the joy of communion in small, support-group Bible studies. Support groups take their basis from 1 Peter 4:8: "Above all hold unfailing your love for one another, since love covers a multitude of sins." Small group Bible studies, usually from six to ten people, meet together at regular times, usually once a week and no less often than once a month, with a common purpose of discovering and growing together in the abundant life in Jesus Christ. The heart of such a group is friendship, a deep commitment to caring about the needs and well-being of other members. The usual format of such a group, which typically meets for about an hour, is Bible study as the common foundation, expression of needs or concerns for which members will pray regularly until an updating at the next meeting, sharing of answers to prayer which are often kept tabulated on a note sheet, and closing with specific prayers for one another, each member praying for the person on his or her right, for example.

These, then, are three suggestions for fellowship from three different walks of life: family, strangers, and friends. We must each, I believe, find something that works effectively for us to nurture the fruit of joy both in our own lives and in the lives of others. But here a word of caution. More than once I have heard someone complain, as they walked away from an opportunity for fellowship, that "this just doesn't meet my needs." Be very clear on this point: Jesus doesn't call us to gratify our own needs. That is never the source of true joy. Jesus calls us to obedience and service, and with very good reason. He has a joy in store for us far beyond what we think "we need." In obedience and service we are constantly surprised by joy. Why is this? Remember the vertical relationship of fellowship in the Holy Spirit. That's our source, and it can never be depleted. As we reach out to others in Jesus' name, that their joy too may be full, we are like a cup pouring out, but since the cup is nourished by the Holy Spirit, it is always overfull. The supply of the Holy Spirit is inexhaustible. Jesus says, "Good measure, pressed down, shaken together, running over, will be put into your lap. For the measure you give will be the measure you get back" (Luke 6:38).

The key to joy with others, joy as fellowship, begins not with the question "What do I need?" but "What can I do?"

For Discussion

Have you ever noticed how we sometimes make the simplest tasks or activities very complex? At one elementary school some parents from the PTA noticed the kindergarten children playing at recess, having a wonderful time making up their own games, laughing happily as they tried to play jump rope. The parents thought it wonderful that the children played so well and so happily. But, they also thought, shouldn't the PTA organize a Play Committee so that they could organize the children's activities more productively. They weren't sure what "productively" meant, but it seemed to be something important because the term is used a great deal nowadays. Soon an adult worker took charge of the children, leading them in "productive" play. The children were bewildered at first, then competition entered, and finally quarreling. Something had been imposed upon them, and they were not sure how to react to it.

That example can apply to fellowship. We sometimes believe fellowship has to be arranged through committees and be highly organized in order to be "productive." This is a serious misunderstanding of fellowship. Fellowship arises as naturally in a Christian spirit as play arises in the spirit of a child. Furthermore, it is a dangerous view because it makes fellowship the responsibility of some committee. It is the responsibility of every Christian who wants to walk closely in the way of Jesus.

Fellowship should arise naturally and easily in our lives, though we can of course do certain things to assist it. You might, for example, do a quick inventory of Bible study aids to use in your own family devotions. What resources do you have for devotions to make them more lively and meaningful for your family? Share these ideas with others. If you don't know where to start, see the salespeople at a nearby Christian bookstore for advice.

You might also ask yourself how you can reach out to others. Follow the example of Abraham. Do you have an opportunity to help a new person in your neighborhood or to invite neighbors in for coffee?

PEACE
When the Way Grows Dark

At the end of the previous chapter, we began to see how all the fruits of the spirit blossom on the one true vine of love for Jesus. All the fruits are different, but in this most glorious garden of the Lord we see the miracle of them growing on one vine. All the fruits are thus somewhat alike but also distinct. Love is the heart of the true vine. Joy grows from love. Joy provides us peace.

No such vine grows naturally in our world, of course. We might force a hybrid someday of, say, plums and peaches and call it a pleach, but it would be neither a plum nor a peach. This true vine and its spiritual fruit is so remarkable because joy and peace, for example, are related while each remains unique among the spiritual fruits. The lesson here is that spiritual fruit is not of this world but nonetheless flourishes in this world. It is the fruit of the *spirit,* but it is revealed dramatically in real, concrete acts in this world. Of no spiritual fruit, perhaps, is this more true than that of peace.

Jesus made this distinction when he said to his disciples the beautiful words, "Peace I leave with you; my peace I give to you; not as the world gives do I give to you. Let not your hearts be troubled, neither let them be afraid" (John 14:27). To understand this otherworldly peace in the midst of the world, consider what the world offers for peace and the response of the spiritual fruit.

This distinction gains clarity through the story of a man who lived in a land with the strange-sounding name of Uz. He was a good man. He loved God and he abhorred evil. In his righteous walk with God, God blessed him. Seven sons and three daughters he had. Thousands of sheep, and camels, and oxen. The family had rich feasts in their spacious house. And the man thanked God for his blessing and remained faithful to God. There was peace in his house.

Until a certain day when Satan, going to and fro on the earth, saw this man and wanted to destroy his peacefulness. Satan, you see, is the one who broke peace with God, and his separation from peace is eternal. Satan's worldly work is to destroy the peace of the Christian. Satan thought this man a likely target. He wanted to tempt him. And he acquired the Lord's permission to do so.

Yes, once before the Lord had permitted Satan to tempt someone. Satan offered the forbidden fruit, and the eternal peace man had with God was so shattered when Adam and Eve took it that it would require Jesus' blood to restore the peace.

And now it happens again. Like another Adam, this man is tested—and what sorrowful testing! One by one the messengers arrive—panting, heart-stricken, mouthing terrible news. An enemy struck and slaughtered the oxen! Fire from heaven destroyed the sheep and shepherds! The camels are killed, along with their keepers! The messengers arrive, one on the heels of another. And then this woeful message—a windstorm struck your eldest son's house, killing all your sons and daughters!

The Eden-broken peace is broken again. Surely, this man has cause to rail against God. Why me, Lord? But we read this instead: "In all this Job did not sin or charge God with wrong" (Job 1:22).

Now, think about that for a minute. I have known people who have cursed God because they missed a taxicab. And, I must confess, more than once I have turned an accusing prayer toward God as I wondered "Why did it have to turn out like this? This isn't working out at all, Lord."

But there is more to come.

The affliction thus far has been external—a loss of possessions and family. To be sure, the pain of such loss is grievous internal hurt, but now the affliction is directed at Job's own body. From the sole of his feet to the crown of his head, Job breaks out in "loathsome" sores. His body is so riddled with painful afflictions, such a torment of the flesh, that his friends don't even recognize him. Imagine the pain of a deep cut, or of an infection, or of a severe sunburn. Over every inch of his body Job is a fiery crucible of pain. At last Job himself feels utterly cast out, and at last the words of cursing come to his lips: "Let the day perish wherein I was born" (Job 3:3).

Understand that no angelic visitor has informed Job *why* he is suffering. No promise has been made to him that the suffering will soon pass away. His world is simply and abruptly turned from peace to terror, from happiness to sorrow, from joy to torment. Job is living evidence of the words of Paul: "For we are not contending against flesh and blood, but against the principalities, against the powers, against the world rulers of this present darkness, against the spiritual hosts of wickedness in the heavenly places" (Eph. 6:12). Job is in the eye of a maelstrom of divine warfare, and he can scarcely understand the battle plan. He knows only too well, though, that his peace has been shattered, apparently beyond reason, beyond belief, beyond restoration.

Job has three friends who come to comfort him—Eliphaz, Bildad, and Zophar. The three friends suggest counsel that will give Job a reason. Eliphaz, perhaps the most sympathetic and compassionate of Job's friends, encourages him to lean on God's mercy, to remain firm in his battle. But Job's wounds are beyond the touch of such encouragement. How can there be any good, Job wonders, when everything is going bad? What reason can one find to go on living when such unreasonable things happen? When the mind fumbles with clumsy fingers for the reasoning of God, what clear answers emerge? No, Job replies, the peace is broken. What can I mean to God who has forsaken me?

Then Bildad speaks, suggesting that if Job cannot find firm assurance in the present by looking to the future, then perhaps he can learn from the past. Surely we have seen God's hand in the past. Isn't that sufficient assurance? And Job agrees. Yes, God has been good in the past. But what answers can I find *now,* sitting in the dust, devastated and lonely? Who can understand what God is doing *now,* and the loathing that I have for my life *now? Now* is "the land of gloom and chaos, where light is as darkness" (Job 10:22). When one suffers in darkness, it is hard to see any light filtering down from the past or any glimmer ahead in the future.

It is not difficult to sympathize with Job's feeling here, for every Christian, at one time or another, has walked the edge of that spiritual loneliness that so overwhelms Job. Some have just walked its periphery, sensing vaguely the terrible desolation as Satan has tried to lure them also from the peace of God. Some have plunged to the very heart of darkness where Job seems like a blood brother and his desolation seems our desolation. There one prays for even a glimmer of light, for the whisper of a star's light on the horizon, and one despairs of ever seeing the full light of spiritual sunshine again. That is precisely where Job is here. The darkness has overwhelmed him and he seems to be fumbling in tight little circles that close more and more narrowly in upon him.

Job's third friend, Zophar, simply loses patience with this. He is the one who would use a little shock therapy. Why can't Job just snap out of it? It's all a matter of point of view. Come on, Job! Cheer up, man. Zophar tells Job to get rid of his sin and he will be all right with God. Toughen up and get over it.

How nice it would be if the Christian could simply get a spiritual injection that would cure a loneliness such as Job's. Or perhaps get a vaccine that would prevent it altogether. In point of fact, the Christian is a part of this fallen world, and Satan is still a roaming lion going to and fro seeking whom he may devour. On the sheerly physical level, one may get a vaccine and still become ill. The great American theologian Jonathan Edwards, newly elected as president of Princeton University, went with his students to get a smallpox vaccination. Two months later he was dead from complications of the illness. And one may receive medications for an illness already afflicting the body, but that illness has to be struggled through toward the cure. Chemotherapy, which has been so beneficial in combatting cancer, in itself causes acute pain and discomfort. No, Zophar, there are no quick and easy cures for Job. He cannot just "snap out of it."

Now, Job's friends are well-intentioned, and there is a degree of truth in each of the things they say. Yes, Eliphaz, one does have to lean on God's mercy. But sometimes one doesn't even have the strength to lean. Yes, Bildad, one does take solace from the past and from a future hope. But can't something be done about the present? And yes, Zophar, one does have to battle against the darkness. But how about when the darkness has you pinned down in an olympic-style wrestling hold and you can hardly breathe, much less fight back? A degree of truth appears in each suggestion, but finally each is insufficient. Why?

Because each focuses upon Job and is dependent upon *his* action. Each sees the answer coming from Job to God. What a mistake! Finally the answer comes from God to Job. The lesson here is the same one recorded in Ephesians 2:8-9: "For by grace you have been saved through faith; and this is not your own doing, it is the gift of God—not because of works, lest any man should boast." Our peace begins and ends in God's will and, although we will work in that will, our peace is not of our own doing but is from God alone.

A marvelous reassurance emanates from that truth, one that can lighten the deepest night of physical or spiritual affliction. Consider this. You have just begun a new job. On the first day of work the boss gives you an envelope, which he tells you to open and use any time. You dutifully go about your work, and get so busy that you forget that envelope in your pocket. Days of hard labor go by. Then one day you fall sick. You become bedridden. The debts pile up and you begin to wonder about paying your bills or even keeping your job. Then one day you remember that envelope. You open it and discover a check for ten thousand dollars. It has been there all the time. All you had to do was to claim it by signing your name to it. Similarly, we have been given a job to do in God's kingdom, but his peace is there waiting for our claim and endorsement.

But that peace is not limited to ten thousand dollars' worth. There is no ceiling on this account. Isaiah 26:3 tells us that "Thou dost keep him in perfect peace, whose mind is stayed on thee, because he trusts in thee." That is peace without limit, without ceiling, without end, because it is the eternal peace of God.

That shapes the lesson for Job. He has been taught a lesson in the inadequacy of human peace and peace according to human understanding. Now it is time for a lesson in God's power and God's peace.

This final lesson begins when Job learns where to turn from the misery of his way to God's way. At first he seems to see only darkness: "Oh, that I knew where I might find him, that I might come even to his seat!" (Job 23:3). But the testimony of Scripture is that God will be found by those who seek him when they seek him with all their heart. As Job probes his darkness for God, he realizes that all human answers are insufficient. And then a new figure comes on the scene: Elihu. And he is angry because all the discourse so far has been on human terms. Elihu is a young man, but here before his elders he boldly proclaims the way of reverence and obedience before God. In one of the most beautiful and moving speeches in the Bible, the young man Elihu asserts the absolute power and majesty of God. Herein lies the Christian peace: that our Lord Omnipotent reigns, that in him alone is the light we seek, and that when all human understanding fails us, God has an answer for us.

Upon this moving proclamation God himself answers Job. Out of the whirlwind God proclaims his majesty and power. And they are thrilling words:

> Where were you when I laid the foundation of the earth?
>   Tell me, if you have understanding.
> Who determined its measurements—surely you know!
>   Or who stretched the line upon it?
> On what were its bases sunk,
>   or who laid its cornerstone,
> when the morning stars sang together,
>   and all the sons of God shouted for joy?
>
> Job 38:4-7

Here is the First Light, the Giver of light, speaking in authority and majesty.

The voice of God does not always come out of the whirlwind or from a burning bush or from the mountaintop. Sometimes it comes, as to Elijah, in a still, small voice saying simply, I am God, and I am here. But therein lies the Christian's peace. The Lord of heaven and earth, the Maker of Light, still reigns in our darkness.

The story of Job has a happy ending. Job repents and God restores his fortune. He is blessed in his latter days beyond the former days. The Christian story has a happy ending also. Because the Maker of Light entered the deepest gulf of our darkness on Calvary, we have an eternal light to guide our way. Because Jesus walked among men and said "Peace, be still," we still have a peacemaker to lighten our way. Every Christian's story has a happy ending; that is the promise of his perfect peace to those whose hearts are stayed on him.

For Discussion

Sometimes we do not have peace because we are afraid of certain things. And there seem to be so many things to fear: physical illness, accidents, psychological suffering, rejection. . . . The list goes on and on.

But is fear always a bad thing? Under what circumstances might fear be a good thing?

Think of a fear you may have had as a child. How did you overcome that fear or begin to view it differently as you grew up?

Many people have needless, unfounded fears, which is commonly called anxiety. For example, one person may believe *his* home is burning each time he hears a siren. Another person believes she has a serious illness each time she feels pain. Although such fears are unfounded, the anxiety they cause is real enough. What promises in the Bible can help allay such anxiety?

CHAPTER TWELVE

PEACE
Along the Way to Peace

"The wisdom of a prudent man is to discern his way" wrote Solomon in Proverbs 14:8.

That is no small task—to discern the way—for Scripture teaches that two ways always lie before us. In fact, Scripture abounds in travel imagery as analogy for the Christian life. Jesus spoke of the narrow way, the one that not everyone travels, the one away from the broad thoroughfare of the worldly crowd. The choice of the right way is terribly important, for along one path lies God's blessing and peace, and along the other path lies the ultimate terror of destruction and God's curse. In Romans 3:16 Paul tells us that "in their paths are ruin and misery" who pursue the broad worldly way.

That way seems bright and alluring to us. It is well posted with all the gaudy and tempting attractions this world has to offer— fame, success, money, comfort. The curious thing about this way, brightly lit as it is with the advertised sensations of the world, is that it slopes downhill. One can never get to the next roadside attraction quickly enough. One begins to stumble downhill, and plunges finally into the jaws of destruction. The words of the prophet Hosea ring along the avenue: "I will punish them for their ways" (Hos. 4:9). It is a slippery slope, and it becomes nearly impossible to climb back out.

Unless, that is, someone builds a bridge out—and that Jesus did. The bridge leads to a different way, a narrow way, a way that is sometimes lonely, a way over which the darkness of Calvary sometimes hovers. There are bends and turns, like the eye of a needle, that one can scarcely slip through. Few bright lights adorn this way; there may be no more than just a few people holding candles to encourage you along. But something special distinguishes this way. As you go further, it does grow easier. You discover Jesus' grace reaching out to hold you as you reach out to him. Above all, for those who travel this way there is the promise of peace. Even when the way grows pinched and narrow—indeed, especially when it seems hardest—grace abounds and God holds the traveler secure.

This is not just a scriptural analogy; it is a promise on which the Bible and the Christian life are structured. To appreciate that more fully, consider seven biblical passages that I believe to be among the most comforting in the Bible. These are promises of God to his children who walk his way.

1

For I know the plans I have for you, says the Lord, plans for welfare and not for evil, to give you a future and a hope. Then you will call upon me and come and pray to me, and I will hear you. You will seek me and find me; when you seek me with all your heart, I will be found by you, says the Lord.

                                                        Jeremiah 29:11-14a

These moving words from Jeremiah were written to the exiles that Nebuchadnezzar had taken to Babylon, to a people wrested from their homeland and stripped of their hope. They were people walking in an unknown way, and Jeremiah reminded them that the Lord knew their way, for he had prepared it. The beautiful testimony and assuring comfort of these words lie in Jeremiah's promise that when people reach out to God, God also, at that same moment, reaches out to them.

It is very hard, of course, to speak to someone's back, and most people have experienced that lonely feeling of trying to talk to someone who has "turned his back" on them. We can imagine how pleased we would be if that person suddenly turned back *to* us, face expectant and eager to hear what we have to say—the prodigal returning with arms open wide. Of course, like the father of the prodigal son, we would rejoice. Jeremiah's promise is that God waits with arms open wide to receive those who seek him with all their heart. This is a common theme in the Bible. We find it in 2 Chronicles 7:14 and again in the words of Jesus.

But even beyond the glorious picture of a waiting, patient God comes the promise of Jeremiah that God has a better way prepared for us. He has plans for our welfare and hope. He has a future for us. But we cannot walk in the way of peace until we turn and walk toward God.

2

You shall not be in dread of them; for the Lord your God is in the midst of you, a great and terrible God.

Deuteronomy 7:21

Peace comes to the one whose heart and mind is stayed on God. But in all honesty we confess that we are human, that our hearts and minds grow fearful, that our seeking of God wavers.

This word of Moses came to the children of Israel as they faced frightening obstacles on their way to the promised land. So many nations stood against them. Their prayers seemed a whisper against the roar of the enemy. But here God said to them that they need not be afraid, for the Lord Almighty over heaven and earth was *in the midst* of them. This is not a god of the distances, a god out there somewhere. Ours is a God among his people, the same God who would become Jesus, the Immanuel, the God with us. Unlike all other gods, remote from the people, our God is a present God. We have no more cause to dread than did the Israelites, for the same eternal God is in the midst of us.

This same theme is echoed in Psalm 90, in which Moses testifies that God "hast been our dwelling place in all generations." God remains our dwelling place in this life, until in the next life we arrive at the mansion that Jesus said he has prepared for us.

3

*Whatever you ask in my name, I will do it, that the Father may be
glorified in the Son; if you ask anything in my name, I will do it.*

John 14:13-14

The two passages from the Old Testament I have already cited
provide us peace in the promises (1) that when we reach out to
God, he reaches out to us, and (2) that God is in our midst
serving as our protector. As fulfillment of God's promise, his
reaching out to us and his being in the midst of us, Jesus opens
all the power of heaven and earth to believers by promising that
"if you ask anything in my name, I will do it."

I earnestly believe that promise. I earnestly believe that Jesus
glorifies the Father in that promise. I also believe that we don't
always pray as Jesus tells us to pray. How astonished I have been
at times by the prayers of my own children! Sometimes they
have prayed with stunning faithfulness and complete trust that
Jesus will heal their friend, for example. But equally astonishing
is this fact—that they, like me, like all humans, sometimes let
human nature govern the prayer. So I shouldn't be surprised,
for example, when one of them prays for something that will
simply be convenient, nice, or pleasant for them.

Now, I also believe that Jesus wants us to have "nice" or "pleasant" times, but sometimes our human nature wants to be the
accelerator that pushes God into overdrive in meeting our
needs. Sometimes, I'm afraid, Christians even use prayer as a
kind of manipulation: "Lord, if you let me have . . . well, then,
I'll. . . ." And then we wonder why the prayer isn't answered as
we *want it to be.*

First of all, every earnest prayer is answered. The promise of
God is that he will hear the believer. Sometimes his answer isn't
what we "want," but it is always better than what we want because
it is his will. As we have already seen, Jeremiah 29:11-14 tells us
that God has a future and a hope for us. We don't know the
future or God's hope for us; we simply believe that he knows it
and that he acts to ensure our future, hope, and welfare. That in
itself is a promise of marvelous peace.

But a second thought comes to bear on this promise of Jesus. He says that anything we ask *in his name* he will do. Our prayers, then, are not to be in our own will, but in Jesus' will. Further, we must ask in our prayers to glorify God, not ourselves. In Gethsemane Jesus himself prayed that not his will but the Father's will be done. If we pray with these two guidelines in mind—that our prayers be in Jesus' name or according to his will and that whatever we ask glorifies the Father—we can be sure that our requests will be granted.

Jesus has promised, furthermore, that he will intercede with the Father that such prayers will be granted. What might such prayers be? What is the example of Jesus? He prayed for healing, for cleansing, for conversion of hearts, for his enemies, for the little children, for his friends. Each of the miracles of Jesus may be considered a prayer. The New Testament itself is the guideline for praying in Jesus' will.

4

Peace I leave with you; my peace I give to you; not as the world gives do I give to you. Let not your hearts be troubled, neither let them be afraid.

John 14:27

On the slippery slope that is the way of the world, it seems that each newly acquired success slips through one's hands even before it can be firmly grasped. Fame? It is eclipsed by someone else's success the following evening. Financial gain? It is eclipsed by new desires. On the slippery slope there is a longing for something that endures, some rock of refuge that won't move when everything else is shaken loose. The things the world gives us seem to have strings attached; they are withdrawn even as we reach for them. Or they break like fragile toys.

Jesus knew this world well and, really, his world of Galilee was not so terribly different from ours. Knowing the nature of the world's way, he offers a gift along his way that never fails, that never changes, that cannot be shaken loose because it is fixed on the rock of Jesus' eternal Godhood. He gives what the world longs for: peace.

Almost echoing Jesus' words, Paul offered comfort to the church at Philippi in the following manner:

> The Lord is at hand. Have no anxiety about anything, but in everything by prayer and supplication with thanksgiving let your requests be made known to God. And the peace of God, which passes all understanding, will keep your hearts and your minds in Christ Jesus.   Philippians 4:5-7

Notice the rich affirmation of this passage. Its promise is predicated entirely upon the God Immanuel—the Lord at hand. Because of Jesus, we should have no anxiety about anything. Because he has promised to hear our prayers, we should pray to him. And in response, he blesses us with the inestimable gift of his peace.

5

In all these things we are more than conquerors through him who loved us. For I am sure that neither death, nor life, nor angels, nor principalities, nor things present, nor things to come, nor powers, nor height, nor depth, nor anything else in all creation, will be able to separate us from the love of God in Christ Jesus our Lord.
                                                  Romans 8:37-39

In the peace-bringing Scripture passages we have just looked at, we see that God calls his people to himself, promising that he will reach out to them as they reach out to God, that those who reach out to God need not have any fear, for God is in the midst of them, that Jesus has promised to answer our prayers, and that his most comforting promise is his peace—not the peace the world offers but the peace the almighty and eternal God gives. Here Paul assures us of victory in Jesus. No matter what befalls us, no matter what oppresses us, we are more than conquerors. We are victorious in the King of kings. So often in our human lives, while trying to walk that narrow way, we are tempted to ask, How long, Lord? When the way grows dim and our knees begin to ache and our spirit hurts, we may wonder, How long, Lord? God has not only promised to lift up the weak knees of those who kneel before him but has promised that we will soar on the wings of eagles. Nothing can separate us from the love of Jesus.

6

And I heard every creature in heaven and on earth and under the earth and in the sea, and all therein, saying, "To him who sits upon the throne and to the Lamb be blessing and honor and glory and might for ever and ever!"

Revelation 5:13

As we walk the narrow way that Jesus describes, it is important to remember where that way finally ends.

Nothing is quite so frustrating as being lost. While camping in the north woods of Michigan once, my children and I ventured far out into the forest. Delighted with the spectacular beauty of the sun-dappled forest floor, wild violets scattered among leaves, a deer we startled at a rushing brook, we kept wandering until we realized we had wandered too far. Now, I have discovered that nothing is harder than finding your way in the forest when the sun is overhead. True, we could have waited until evening and then followed the sun's direction somewhere back to our lost camp. But at midday every slant of light looks the same, and an afternoon is a long time to wait. Especially for children who are already missing lunch. One of my daughters suggested looking at moss on trees—we knew our camp lay to the south. But in the deep forests of the Michigan north woods, moss is governed by moisture, not light. Moss grows almost uniformly around the huge trunks. An unpleasant feeling, being lost.

How did we get out? One of us, I forget who, remembered that a stream flowed by our camp. Could it be the same one at which we had seen the deer drinking? It was. We followed its winding path back to a waiting lunch.

The special comfort of Revelation 5:13 is that the Christian way arrives not just at a temporary camp but at our true home. It is a place where we know that all our seeking is rewarded beyond our wildest hopes and dreams because the way ends at the throne of Jesus, the place where everyone must eventually pass, where every knee shall bend and every tongue confess that Jesus is Lord, but it is also the final resting place on the Christian pilgrimage.

7

There shall no more be anything accursed, but the throne of God and of the Lamb shall be in it, and his servants shall worship him; they shall see his face, and his name shall be on their foreheads. And night shall be no more; they need no light of lamp or sun, for the Lord God will be their light, and they shall reign for ever and ever.

Revelation 22:3-5

The beauty of the Christian way is that it leads surely and fruitfully to the throne of the Lamb of God, who reigns forever. But that way opens into a vast and glorious place. There will not be anything accursed there—no illness, no pain either physical or spiritual, no crime, no fear. And especially no darkness, for this vast place is lit by the eternal light of God Almighty. We are told in Revelation 21:4 that God himself will wipe the tears from our eyes. Imagine that: no tears in heaven! No sorrow!

There are times, we admit, when our way seems dark. But these things shall all pass away. They are called by John "the former things" for our memories will be healed of them in the Lamb's place. At that place, to which we are steadily walking, only the bright Morning Star shall shine.

Buchenwald is still a name that evokes a chill of horror among any with a sense of history. Built in 1937, when Hitler began to swing an iron fist of destruction and extermination over the Jews, Buchenwald was the first and the model concentration camp—a model for terrifying genocide. In November of 1938, ten thousand Jews were shipped to Buchenwald, the first in a long line of prisoners that would eventually number in the millions. Here the Germans inflicted incredible horrors upon the prisoners, literally working them to death, starving them, torturing them, experimenting with drugs and chemicals upon them. The nearby crematoriums burned around the clock. For over fifty thousand prisoners, Buchenwald was a death camp. The road that led to Buchenwald was a broad road of destruction.

Today another road passes near Buchenwald. It is called the Freedom Highway. Cars scurry along its paved lanes, but in the background looms the mute testimony of the horror that was Buchenwald.

Side by side, two roads: one the death road, the way of tyranny and cruelty, the other the way of freedom. In "The Road Not Taken," Robert Frost writes,

> I shall be telling this with a sigh
> Somewhere ages and ages hence:
> Two roads diverged in a wood, and I—
> I took the one less traveled by,
> And that has made all the difference.

There is a broad spiritual path that leads to destruction and terror, and there is a narrower spiritual path that is the freedom road. Can we, like Frost, say we took the one less traveled by? That choice makes all the difference.

For Discussion

If peace is a fruit of the spirit, that fruit also needs to be nurtured. Identify one area of your life in which you must particularly pray for and nurture the fruit of peace.

Is there a relationship with an individual that needs healing, where peace must be restored? Pray specifically for that relationship.

To be peacebringers to others, Christians must first of all be at peace with themselves and with God. Sometimes hurting memories must also be healed. This too can be brought to prayer.

Since Jesus is the pattern for our Christian walk, we do well to think of specific actions of Jesus that restored peace. What examples arise in Matthew 6:25-27 and 26:50-54?

CHAPTER THIRTEEN

PATIENCE
How Long, Lord?

Let me put this bluntly. Patience is the most tragically misunderstood fruit of the spirit. Perhaps for that very reason, it may also be one of the most profoundly important.

Because of the misunderstanding and importance of patience in the Christian life, consider these points. Remembering our analogy to gardening, impatience is the weed that must be rooted out. But equally important is the point that patience is *not* simply doing nothing at all: it is not inaction. Properly understood, patience is an active, dynamic, involved way of living.

Impatience is probably one of the most common human weeds, but whenever I think of impatience, a boyhood scene rises in my mind. I was raised in a huge old house, full of sprawling rooms and interesting nooks and crannies. On the second floor of the back wing of the house was my summer bedroom. This spacious room had nine windows, three on each of its open sides, which created a pleasant breeze in even the hottest Michigan months. But in winter that breeze became a blue-nosed draft, and so by late October each year I would move to a smaller bedroom for the winter months.

Late October was also about the time my parents started wrapping Christmas presents and storing them in the "big room," my vacated summer bedroom. Since the huge room was almost impossible to heat, the heat was cut off altogether, kept just above freezing level by the warmth rising from the lower story. It was bone-chilling cold when I would creep in there and gaze upon those brightly wrapped packages, to touch this one, to give that one a gentle shake to see if anything rattled. I couldn't resist. When the house was quiet, I would slip in. But each time I did, a current of cold air would cascade down the hall, announcing my truancy to my parents below.

"You're not in the big room again, are you?" I would hear. And quickly shutting the door, I would call back, "Not anymore!"

Now this was a persecution greater than one boy should have to bear. To know those gifts were only a closed door, albeit a cold one, away! To know they would stay there until precisely 6 A.M. on Christmas morning—not one minute before, although I would be lying awake half the night! That was a strain on patience, I was convinced, I would never be able to endure.

Yet each year, my parents made sure that I did.

I wanted those things on my timetable. That package I was sure I recognized as a model airplane—I could so nicely work on that now! Indeed, it seems a fundamental quality of human nature to want things now. We live in anticipation of things to come, and each new thing is *overcome* by another anticipation.

James clearly speaks about this in his New Testament letter. The Christian church then was also living in anticipation—and impatience. They were undergoing persecution, and they looked for the return of the Lord—*now*—to end it all. Three times in the space of two verses James encourages the church to *be patient:* "Be patient, therefore, brethren, until the coming of the Lord. Behold, the farmer waits for the precious fruit of the earth, being patient over it until it receives the early and the late rain. You also be patient. Establish your hearts, for the coming of the Lord is at hand" (James 5:7-8). A world of teaching resides in those two verses.

In verse 7, James tells us to be patient "therefore." Therefore? On account of what? *Therefore* always signals a conclusion from certain premises. These premises are supplied by James in the preceding six verses. To the church at that time it seemed that there was no justice, and they were impatient because of it. The rich and the persecutors seemed to grow ever more powerful, while the faithful struggled to the day of the Lord which never seemed near at hand. In those first six verses James reminds them that God has *his* calendar. We don't know the dates affixed to it; we can only be certain of his promises, among them the promise that oppression will come to an end. Since we don't know God's calendar, James encourages us to be patient in our calendar.

Then he raises an interesting analogy for human and spiritual patience: "the farmer waits for the precious fruit of the earth, being patient over it until it receives the early and the late rain." This is a loaded little passage. The farmer has confidence. He does not simply wait for something to happen, but for the "precious fruit." He knows that he must wait out the interval until the harvest. But what kind of farmer would wait by doing nothing? Because he believes that the fruit will be precious, he works daily in the field weeding and nurturing that fruit. Waiting is not doing nothing. It is doing what you can, and all that you can, with the realization that the final authority lies elsewhere.

Notice the second significant item in that verse: the farmer waits until the crop has received the early *and* the late rain—both the starting rain and the maturing rain. All kinds of impatience come to bear on gardening and farming. One afternoon some little boys plant a packet of seeds and the next day they dig them all up to see if they're growing. But other gardeners are not far short of the little boys. How many haven't picked the crop before it fully matured, thereby robbing themselves of the full "preciousness" of the crop? The good farmer waits for the late rain also.

But notice that the farmer has no control over the rain. This is in God's calendar. Until the late rains come to mature the fruit, the farmer works at the task at hand to prepare for it, and in so working he earnestly believes in the coming of the precious crop.

On the one hand, then, we have impatience as the counterpart to Christian patience, and this covers a broad range of things in our personal lives—impatience with family members, impatience to achieve expected goals, impatience in awaiting answers to prayer. But again, patience should not be understood as doing nothing at all. Remember the farmer's active and energetic "waiting."

This is a lesson poorly learned by modern Christians. Too

often we exercise patience by doing nothing. It is profoundly disheartening how many Christians have simply given up the struggle, how many have equated patience with mere resignation. It is fearfully hard to work in the garden of the world to nurture God's precious crop. So often our one voice seems a whisper against the roar of corruption and the thunderous silence of indifference. But we cannot be silent. In this world, more than ever, *active* patience is called for.

Let me give one example. I and my family have actively involved ourselves in the struggle against abortion for more years than I dare remember. We have always done so peaceably, even when the frustration mounts. We do so because we believe that the Word of God is unequivocal on the issue. There are six things that the Lord hates, says Solomon, seven which are an abomination to him. And one of these is the shedding of innocent blood (Prov. 6:16-17).

The method of struggle is equally clear in Scripture: we must struggle in Jesus' way, the way of servanthood. Servanthood to God recognizes a sin and acts to correct it, but it loves the sinner. We must do everything possible to create a moral climate that affirms the value of families and children, to delight in our family without apology and with pride, and to understand that that family includes those without family, those who are single, those born out of wedlock. We must do everything possible to support the woman who has had an abortion. After having received the touch of loss, she desperately needs the touch of love. Servanthood gives it to her, and it also extends it to those who are apparently thoroughly at ease with their actions, including the father who has turned his back, or has had his back turned, on his unborn child.

In servanthood we must do everything possible, furthermore, to rely on the Lord and engage in prayer, including, as Jesus urged, prayer for those who mistreat us and despitefully use us. That takes patience. I do believe that we should pray about issues of life without ceasing, and that prayer will move the mountain of indifference.

Saying this, I am well aware that we who struggle wonder, How long, Lord? As the numbers of the slain unborn and now the barely born mount, we wonder, How long, Lord? If those eighteen million names were engraved on the Vietnam Veterans Memorial, that monument would stretch from the Lincoln Memorial nearly to the very steps of the Supreme Court itself. I am a veteran of the Vietnam War, drafted from graduate school in 1968. Twice now I have stood at the foot of that monument and a chill that was not from the weather swept through me and tears which were not from the wind came to my eyes. During that year I thought daily, How long, Lord? And that imaginary monument rises in my mind, stretching from the Lincoln Memorial to the steps of the Supreme Court, engraved with eighteen million names known only to God, and I say, How long, Lord? And he asks each of us the same question.

Yes, be patient in the Lord. His calendar is not our calendar; his days and ways not our days and ways. But, as Paul said in Romans 2:7, be patient *in well-doing*. This is active patience. Our patience, finally, does not rest in things of this world but in Jesus. Until that time, however, when his eternal kingdom comes to pass and the calendar as we know it is subsumed in his eternal calendar, we will work to redeem the "precious fruit" of this world he has given into our hands. Those hands are not expected to be, nor can they be, indifferent and idle.

For Discussion

In our reflections in Chapter Nine, we saw that there are clear biblical directions for dealing with social issues in a Christian way. Read the eighth chapter of Amos, that great book on social issues, particularly verses 4-12. What clear principles does God set down in this brief passage?

Some say that we should separate *social* issues from *moral* issues. Can the Christian do this? Aren't all social issues ultimately moral issues? How do some modern thinkers, particularly in politics and law, try to separate them?

How do we respond to world hunger? One important responsibility is to inform ourselves so that we know the need and can respond to it. For example, it is estimated that ten million children in the third world countries are going blind because of vitamin deficiencies. A dosage of vitamin A administered twice a year can prevent such blindness. How long can we package such needs out of our minds?

CHAPTER FOURTEEN

PATIENCE
Grace and Confidence

On the far reaches of the northern peninsula of Michigan, a strange, almost mystical jut of land stretches into the heart of Lake Superior. It is called the Keweenaw Peninsula, one of the most fascinating stretches of land in the United States. All kinds of natural and human barriers lie in the path of a traveler to the Keweenaw.

The natural barriers are there. The weather in this region is so changeable that one is hard-pressed to believe any pattern reigns. Keweenaw veterans have a favorite saying: "Don't like the weather? Stick around an hour; it'll change." This is true, in fact, for much of Michigan's upper peninsula. I have stood at the Soo Locks watching huge vessels angle delicately through the narrow slips in a cold drizzle with a daytime high of 50 degrees in the middle of July, and a day later camped under a warm sun only a hundred miles west. It is even more changeable in the little jut of land that is Keweenaw. Near the tip of the peninsula a snow marker that measures annual snowfall rises along the highway. The top of the marker rises above the telephone wires and poles. The average annual snowfall is 176 inches—nearly fifteen feet of snow. The record year, 1978-79, saw 390 inches of snow—thirty-two and a half feet! To cross the upper peninsula, you pass through hills of such startling beauty you hold your breath in awe, and also through wasteland so wild and empty you think you are traveling the face of some distant planet. The land unfolds with startling contrasts.

Indeed, it takes a high degree of patience to travel in the upper peninsula and especially all the way to Keweenaw. Just getting someplace in the upper peninsula is a challenge. The roads are among the worst I have ever traveled, roller coasters sprawling across the tortured hills. But for one with the patience, there waits a reward that can only be described as grace. Camped on the high bluffs of McLain State Park, overlooking the huge expanse of Lake Superior, one begins to feel a sense of reverence. In mid-July the sun sets around 11 P.M., a globe of crimson that washes the water and casts a purple nimbus around Isle Royale, lying forty-five miles offshore. Near Copper Harbor one passes rugged waterfalls of breathtaking beauty that aren't even advertised in travel brochures. The two-lane road dips through meadows choked with flowers—goldenrod, daisies, and lupine. One rises to high peaks laced with paper-white birch, surrounded by the song of a thousand birds, and sees Superior sprawled below like a blue gem. It takes patience getting there, but the reward is grace.

And if one travels south toward Ironwood, another surprise awaits. The road winds casually through small mining towns, around and over tumbling mountains. Nearing Ontonagon State Park, one begins thinking of bears. The park is famous for them, and backpackers routinely return with stories of raids that end with the bears running off with a bellyful of food.

A thin road winds from the campground up a mountainside, stretching higher and higher above Lake Superior until the horizon seems a clear blue line curved around the rim of the world. After a series of hairpin turns, the road dead-ends and the last few hundred yards have to be taken afoot. The climb takes some endurance, if not patience, but a spectacular scene awaits the climber at the rim: there in the great bowl of the mountaintop hundreds of feet below is "Lake of the Clouds," a secret blue jewel dropped in a bed of emerald-green pine. Again, one feels the urge to kneel and worship; one begins to understand grace.

That understanding is also essential to understanding patience. Christian patience roots not in our own life and action but in God's grace to us. We can be patient because God has been patient and gracious to us. We can endure the hard roads of life because God has shaped the way. The very key to patience lies in the knowledge that our goal is not rooted in this life but in eternal life. This assurance is underscored in the letter to the Thessalonians: "May the Lord direct your hearts to the love of God and to the steadfastness of Christ" (2 Thess. 3:5). Our patience here is modeled upon the eternal steadfastness of Jesus. Even if a goal does not appear immediately clear to us, we can still be patient. As Paul puts it, "if we hope for what we do not see, we wait for it with patience" (Rom. 8:25).

But that expectation may also be flipped around. Because we live this life in terms of eternal life, we are also representing things eternal, are in fact representing Jesus himself, to people in this life. As Christians we are Christ-like, human agents of his divine patience and grace.

Surely we become impatient with wickedness in our time. Yet David counsels us to "be still before the Lord, and wait patiently for him; fret not yourself over him who prospers in his way, over the man who carries out evil devices" (Ps. 37:7). What then is patience? It is a steadfast certainty, first of all, that God is in control. Second, the motivation and power for patience rests in the knowledge that God has a gracious answer for us beyond our expectation and fondest hope. Third, patience is the knowledge that in this life we are representing Jesus to others and should exemplify the same humility and patience he has shown.

Understood in this way, patience is not simply a stoic endurance, a hard-eyed, gritted-teeth "seeing the thing through." Patience is calm assurance, being at peace in whatever storm, because our eternal hope rests in Jesus and not in things of this world. Patience may best be understood, then, as confidence. It derives from strength, not from weakness. It acts according to the certainty of love, joy, and peace.

Patience is a hard fruit to nurture. Human psychology (we want what we want when we want it) and human events work against it. As with the other fruits, hard storms assail our patience, creating times when we are at a loss for sure, neat answers. This lesson also might be reviewed in the north woods of Michigan.

Pause by a stream and notice the interplay, the choir, of sounds. Sudden differences jar the murmur of the stream; the sweet notes of a cardinal flute on and on, over and over. Something moves in the far brush and the thudding you hear is your own heart. The breeze wisps lazily through leaves and sends light slanting along the forest floor. And you begin to notice: here it is again, life being reduced to its small parts, to stillnesses between gusts of wind, to silences between sounds.

Stay here by the stream and notice next the colors. At first the deep forest seems a haze of gray-green. But the gray wash of the hurried glance breaks apart, receives distinction as you look, and look again. Look first at the high colors so that your eye moves with the light. Above, a million or more high needles of white pine spear the light in points of amber and red and silver. Leaves of poplar and beech cast the light shimmering along satin gray trunks. The trees are alive with reds that dart out in a flicker of bark, a vein of a leaf. Along the forest floor shades of green skip and dance. You look closer now, notice for the first time the clump of trillium. In a leaffall the thin orange fingers of the coral mushroom feel the air. Along a rotten log propped against a pine, a sprawling sulphur shelf fungus, white with pink edges and a green belly, lies like a small beast panting. The fragrant pink cups of a wild rose hedge the trunk of the pine. The forest floor is a litter of red and brown needles, knit by the spindling shape of a blue racer that flails the shadows.

And this sight, which is unmatched in the north woods for its beauty and sudden grace: the brush in the background shadows of two large trees that you have looked at, trying to decipher its peculiar shape, suddenly parts. The majestic antlered head of the deer turns toward you—or, rather, toward the sound you have made—and suddenly the great body leaps, the white tail high and bounding as the deer disappears.

The deer provides a particular loveliness to the north woods, and it may often be seen if you are quiet and patient, willing to become one with the sights and sounds of the forest, to become a pilgrim. Wait at sunrise and you may see the water-backed fawn, shiny with dew, bend on its spraddled legs to this very stream, the large doe waiting by the brush while the fawn drinks. Often you may see the doe, three or four at a time, poling the ground on their springy legs.

It is a sight we never weary of, that we grow impatient for. Especially this other time in the north woods.

Winter holds a special call to the heart attuned to the north

woods. Sunlight spills more freely across the forest floor, startling strange shapes of wind and snow. An ogre looms behind a
twisted trunk. A vaporous spirit skids across the broken face of
the stream. Winter is the magic time in the north woods, a time
when this forever unfamiliar world becomes the wholly other
world of fantasy.

The air this day had the sharp bite of five below, breath crack-
ling in the air and forming frosting on the mufflers, sounds as
clear as a cardinal's call.

My youngest daughter saw them first: crisp, twin-toed tracks
in the snow edging cautiously, almost daintily, out from the
brush. And for no better reason than that it was five below and
the world a frozen bed of winter's sleep, we thought we would
startle a dream in the north woods. We would follow the tracks,
find the deer like a pot of gold at their end.

The snow swept evenly through the forest as if laid down in a
single, smooth stroke, disturbed only at one awkward angle
where the diamond-backed stream hurried in its winter bed. We
paused by the ice-edged water, and went up the bank on the
other side. We crossed and followed.

We followed the tracks from a brushfall to the downed trunk
of an oak. We noted where the deer leaped, ran, stood silent,
pawed at the snow to get at grass or twigs. We began to imagine
it standing before us, snuffing the air, head cocked backward to
keep us in view, then disappearing in a flash of white while we
hurried in its tracks.

The trail led us at length to a clearing. I should have known
the signs; perhaps, like a good soldier knowing himself de-
feated, I should have retreated then. But this was where the
tracks led, and she wanted to follow.

A switchback of boards was nailed in the crotch of a pine; its
evergreen boughs a veil between the clumsy seat and the clearing. A ladder pointed gray fingers up the trunk. No one could
have missed these signs. Beneath the sweeping limbs of the pine
were arranged a manger-sized bundle of hay and many overripe
apples, frozen hard, wearing thin, lacy-white skins of frost.

Propped against the snowbank stood—immobile, softly tufted
with dark, downy hair—the two hind feet of the deer, the white

shanks of bone protruding through a red collar just above the ankle joint.

I suppose the hunter had meant them to mark his particular blind. Perhaps they were his sign that he had had enough of hunting now, that the sweet apples and green hay were ready for another. Perhaps he had a gentler side, but it was lost in the questions my daughter was asking.

How can one remain patient when joy and beauty seem sucked out of the world? When rude markers lie in our path, and we stumble over them and hurt ourselves, when all neat answers seem to conflagrate in fiery questions, where can we turn to set our way aright? This is the hard waiting on the Lord, the waiting that touches the hard edge of the call for patience. Here, also, the words of Jesus come alive to us: "My grace is sufficient for you, for my power is made perfect in weakness" (2 Cor. 12:9).

For Discussion

God is the ultimate model for Christian action. Sometimes people look so closely at situations that they lose sight of God. But it is also good to consider how patient God is with his people.

A good example of God's patience is found in Genesis 18 and 19, where we read that Abraham interceded for Sodom because Lot lived there. Sodom was an exceedingly godless and vulgar city. God had every right to obliterate that place, in much the same way that we would want to obliterate a disease before it spreads and infects others. Yet, because of Abraham's intercession, God patiently sent angels to warn Lot and free him from both the sinfulness and destruction.

We can measure the growth and maturity in our Christian lives by identifying the areas in which God has been patient with us. Each of us has caught the disease of sin; else there would be no need for a savior. But patience does not mean doing nothing. Is it legitimate for us to become impatient with our own sin.

What does Paul mean when he says in Hebrews 12:1, "Let us run with patience the race set before us?" Is he talking about a forty-yard dash, or a lifelong cross-country marathon?

In what area of life do you lose patience most quickly, and how can you change that? Can one devise a *plan* for patience?

CHAPTER FIFTEEN

KINDNESS
Leaving Childish Ways

In his timeless story *Alice's Adventures in Wonderland,* Lewis Carroll spins a fascinating tale of one person's journey through unbelievable places. All these places are, however, a little bit like real life. One of the strangest places Alice finds herself is at the edge of the woods where she glances up and sees the Cheshire Cat sitting on the limb of a tree. She is frightened at first, because the cat does indeed have very long claws and a great many sharp teeth, and so she asks him very timidly: "Would you tell me, please, which way I ought to go from here?"

That is not an unusual question, especially since Alice doesn't even know where she is. But the Cheshire Cat responds, "That depends a good deal on where you want to get to." The dialogue that follows is most interesting:

> "I don't much care where . . ." said Alice.
> "Then it doesn't matter which way you go," said the Cat.
> ". . . so long as I get *somewhere,*" Alice added as an explanation.
> "Oh, you're sure to do that," said the Cat, "if you only walk far enough."

This exchange between Alice and the Cheshire Cat establishes an important point. Nurturing the fruit of the spirit must be understood as a way of living. It is not just going *somewhere,* which we are sure to do if only we walk far enough. Such undirected action is as likely to raise weeds as fruit. Nurturing and bearing the fruit of the spirit begins with a commitment in which we prepare our way for the flourishing of the fruit.

Each fruit of the spirit has a counterpart, a weed that must be eradicated. In the case of kindness, it is easy to identify. What chokes kindness? Arrogance, self-centeredness—both words for what may be described more commonly as an "I" infection. This infection, in which the "I" stands at the heart of all a person thinks or does, cannot be cleared up with a few drops in the morning. Kindness may be described as standing outside oneself to see and meet the needs of others. Those afflicted with the "I" infection are incapable of seeing beyond their own wants, needs, and feelings. Perhaps this is what Paul had in mind when he said, "When I was a child, I spoke like a child, I thought like a child, I reasoned like a child; when I became a man, I gave up childish ways" (1 Cor. 13:11). For the child, his own wants, needs, and feelings are the center of the universe, and if he doesn't get what he wants he makes it known at the top of his lungs. Many parents have wondered why the largest organs of a baby are the lungs and voicebox. At least they seem to be, for when the baby lets his needs be known few can mistake it.

The weed of arrogance thinks first of self. Another vicious little counterpart to biblical kindness masquerades as the real fruit. When you taste of it, however, this false fruit is bitter indeed. It may look a little more like the fruit, but it is linked to the weed. We can all identify selfish and arrogant people, but how about the person who seems to act kindly, but only to serve his own ends? This is harder to locate, and since we run the risk of being judgmental if we try to find evidences of it in others, we will do well to look for it first in ourselves. Have I ever done kindnesses for the simple reason that I wanted the hearty thanks, the recognition, or the public praise? We all like to be recognized for our good deeds and to be praised for them. That is a part of human nature. But does that become the primary motivating factor for our kindness? Can we do acts of kindness even knowing that we will receive no praise or thanks for it? Can we do acts of kindness even if it hurts to do them and they will be resented?

A few years ago our city started a Parent Aide Program. Its aim is friendship intercession in child abuse cases. Many child abusers were abused children themselves, caught in a vicious cycle of poor parenting and abuse that is being perpetuated from one generation to the next. My wife, Pat, enrolled as one of the first volunteers in that program designed to provide friends who will also be models for the abusive parent.

After some weeks of training she received her assignment—an immigrant mother whose husband had left her and who was now trying to raise three children, the middle one of which, at the age of thirteen, already had a delinquency record healthier than his report card. The oldest boy of fifteen and the daughter of eight seemed to be the ones trying the hardest to hold the family together. But there were other problems. Although the mother was simply too small a woman to be physically abusive, emotional abuse and neglect were severe. As weeks passed there seemed, however, to be some progress. Pat visited her weekly, and as the relationship grew, our two families took picnics together, visited the zoo or museum, and did other things together. I stayed in the background, occasionally on the scene to chat or chauffeur, but largely out of the picture. Since there was no father in the other family, I was perceived as kind of a threat to the relationship Pat was trying to establish with the other woman.

Sadly enough, the relationship, as it became closer, also grew more strained. As the woman got to know Pat, she began to unload on her. I mean heavily. And as she began to unload on Pat, she also began to resent her, to identify her as part of the problem. We were assured this was not unusual, that it was a process of "objectifying" for the mother: as she got her problems out in the open, she tended to see them in another person. But it made it awfully hard for Pat, who wanted to go as a friend but who was seen as part of the problem when she came. No amount of assurance helps when a person begs you to come and then resents you for being there. Fortunately, having worked for a long time in psychiatric nursing, Pat understood better than I the psychology going on. All I saw was a kindness going unthanked—worse, being resented.

Then came a Saturday night in the dead of winter. We got a phone call from the mother just after we had gone to bed. "I'm dying," she said, and wouldn't talk any further. What did that mean? Was she physically ill? Had she attempted suicide? In her mental condition we knew she was capable of anything. We got a neighbor to watch our children, jumped in the car and drove across town to her house.

It was cold inside. Bitterly cold. It was the first time I had been in the house. It reeked. Odds and ends of anything imaginable lay piled up in corners. The children had winter coats on; the eight-year-old was cooking some food at the stove. The mother was hunched up on the bed like a twisted doll. Had she taken anything? She couldn't answer. We put her in the car and took her to the hospital, leaving the children in the care of the fifteen-year-old until we returned.

Now here's a strange thing about mental hospitals that I have learned: in our city they don't like to admit patients after midnight or on weekends. While we sat with her in the emergency room of the nearest medical hospital, we called three mental hospitals for admission. One could take her Monday morning. The doctor in the emergency room sedated her and we took her home.

We were just back in bed around three A.M. when the phone rang again. "Mama says she's dying."

We contacted a child haven worker. The children would have to go somewhere, after all. They couldn't stay at the house, and we didn't have beds at our house (although we have since added space and have used it often). The child haven worker (appointed by the court) met us there, along with three squad cars in response to the children's frantic calls. By early Sunday morning the mother had been bedded down under sedation at the hospital until she could be placed in a mental hospital, and the children had been taken to a foster care home. The mother left telling Pat she never wanted to see her again.

We heard from her only a few times after that. She refused to talk to Pat when she called, would not admit her to the house when she visited. Even after the children were returned she blamed Pat for taking them away.

A prayer we used to pray when we did door-to-door evangelism ran through our minds often. The gist of it was that you did the best you could do and left the rest for the Holy Spirit. We don't have to win the battles; God will take care of that. He only asks us to keep fighting. Kindness is one of the weapons of the Christian, even when it is not met with thanks, even when it is met with bitterness. There is no earthly reward in that, and no room for "I" infections when we may seem to fail miserably.

Why do deeds of kindness, then? Other fruits of the spirit seem to give us something: love, peace, joy. . . . But this one seems to cost us something. Is that really the case?

Two things figure into the answer. First, out of his kindness alone, God has redeemed us. He didn't owe us anything; or rather, if he owed us anything, it was wrath and retribution. But he gave us—kindness. In Ephesians 2:7 Paul writes that God shows "the immeasurable riches of his grace in kindness toward us in Christ Jesus." That word *grace* is sometimes defined as an acronym of the phrase God's Riches At Christ's Expense. That is divine kindness. And second, by showing kindness to others, we show God's kindness. So we really do get something in nurturing this fruit: the knowledge of God's kindness to us and the privilege of extending it to others. Kindness is something we do for others, not for ourselves, and quite often at the expense of ourselves.

But a caution is in order here. We sometimes think of kindness as the big things we do, the things that we have to go out of our way for. That is a mistake. Take note of the fact once more that each of the fruits of the spirit is a *way of living*, and so too is kindness. Kindness begins in the little things, the way we treat each other in the home, for example. The way we greet each other, talk to each other, do things for each other; these are the starting points for kindness in the family of God.

Recently a minister in a rather conservative denomination told me of a problem he had had early in his ministry. He had started a mission church in a rural community, and every single Tuesday, rain or shine, sleet or snow, a carful of ladies from a large denominational church in a nearby city came to his mission church to teach Bible school to the children. It seemed a happy situation; the children came readily, and the women loved to teach them.

At that particular time, however, this conservative denomination was having a church-wide controversy about the nature of

God's love. One hardly knows how such discussions arise, but arise it did. And it troubled one of the women who came to see the missionary-evangelist with her problem.

"The church is debating whether God loves everyone," said the lady.

"Yes, I suppose it is," responded the evangelist wearily.

"Do you think God loves these children?"

The evangelist was stunned. In the back of his mind was the verse: "God so loved the world . . ." But how to make her see that? "Well," he said, "Tell me. Do you love these children?"

"Oh, yes," she replied.

"And does Jesus love you?"

"Oh, yes," she said. "He died to save me."

"Then don't you think that if Jesus loves you, and you love the children, then Jesus loves the children through you?"

There it was, observed the evangelist, solved, even without a committee to study it. And his point was correct. Jesus loves *through* us. Because of his kindness to us, we show his kindness, gracious, undeserved, and sometimes without thanks, to others.

For Discussion

George MacDonald once wrote that "a man must not choose his neighbor: he must take the neighbor that God sends him. . . . The neighbor is just the man who is next to you at the moment, the man with whom any business has brought you into contact." Jesus' parable about the Good Samaritan is a parable of kindness. But how do we show kindness to our neighbor, the one God has sent to us at this moment?

One way to answer this is to ask this further question: Do those who look at me see Jesus? As Christians we are to be Christ-like, representing Jesus to the world. Can others see the kindness of Jesus in me?

An interesting lesson in kindness was taught to Jonah outside the gates of Nineveh. What does the fourth chapter of Jonah reveal about God's kindness, and about what he expects of us as representatives of his kindness?

CHAPTER SIXTEEN

GOODNESS
A Do-Gooder or Doing Good?

This small brick church standing proudly atop a hill in south-eastern Ohio and commanding a beautiful view of the valley below had a most humble beginning. The church is still new enough to hold the smell of paint and the peculiar scent of fresh carpeting in the small sanctuary. Not very long before this building was finished, much of the labor done by members of the congregation, that same congregation had been meeting in the cattle auction barn on Sunday mornings. The problem was that auctions were held on Saturday, and a great deal of frenzied sweeping and mopping had to be done before Sunday morning worship. But it was a good bargain—the cattle auction people got their barn cleaned, and the congregation had a place to worship.

The auction barn had in fact been a step up for the congregation, since before they started meeting there they had met in the front yard of a farmer. Services were held under the oak tree. That wasn't so bad until one morning a thunderstorm broke in on the sixty worshipers. That impressed them. Even a cattle auction barn was better. And finally this new, brick church—each brick lovingly laid by members of that small congregation.

Much of the motivating force behind this church was the wife of the farmer in whose front yard services were originally held. She didn't like the long drive into town on Sunday mornings, but, more than this, she believed the country folk needed their own place to worship. It was she who had baked cookies and made Kool Aid for the Sunday services in her front yard. She organized the worship in the cattle auction barn. She supplied much of the management, and a good deal of the baking, for the weekend church-raising parties for the new building.

I had the pleasure of worshiping in that church many times, because I was then "a country folk," living on a farm during my graduate school days. And I got to know this remarkable woman quite well. But I particularly remember overhearing a remark one Sunday after worship. Two women were chatting outside the front door, sipping coffee, enjoying the warm April sun and watching the green fields in the valley below. One woman remarked to the other in a loud voice, "Well, just ask Mrs. Cochrane to do it. She's a do-gooder."

The comment cast a kind of pall over the sunny spring morning. Just a "do-gooder." No, not Mrs. Cochrane. She was a woman doing good, committed to a goal and seeing it through to the end, but above all committed to her Lord and doing his good in the world.

That is a point of frequent confusion, however. Is one a "do-gooder," simply doing good things in the world out of a sense of obligation, duty, virtue, or whatever; or is one doing good in the name of the Lord?

The fruit of goodness must be understood above all as "doing the right thing." Goodness has purpose and authority behind it. In fact, to some people it may not even look like good. It is biblically good, for example, to discipline our children, but it may not seem good to them. Goodness may even be doing the unpopular thing, not to please humans but to please God. We may receive no praise from others when we do good—active, committed good—but as Proverbs 12:20 points out, "those who plan good have joy." This joy that is the result of the fruit of goodness comes from the knowledge that in doing good we do the will of the Lord, even when that doing is unpopular, even when it meets with the scorn of others. Perhaps that is what Solomon also had in mind when he wrote that "a perverse man will be filled with the fruit of his ways, and a good man with the fruit of his deeds" (Prov. 14:14).

If we take the teaching of Jesus seriously, we learn that doing good takes considerable daring and courage. In the sixth chapter of Luke, Jesus gives his courageous Law of Love. We are to love God with all our heart and mind and strength, as the prophets said. We are to love our neighbor as ourselves, as the prophets said. But Jesus goes a step beyond the prophets and gives specific direction for the Christian to do good:

> If you love those who love you, what credit is that to you? For even sinners love those who love them. And if you do good to those who do good to you, what credit is that to you? For even sinners do the same. And if you lend to those from whom you hope to receive, what credit is that to you? Even sinners lend to sinners, to receive as much again. But love your enemies, and do good, and lend, expecting nothing in return; and your reward will be great, and you will be sons of the Most High; for he is kind to the ungrateful and the selfish. Be merciful, even as your Father is merciful.
>
> Luke 6:32-36

That, I submit, is one of the most daring pieces of teaching in the Bible. Jesus directs us to do good even in the face of no reward from men. This is not a teaching for mere "do-gooders"; it is a teaching for those who dare to do good. Our model in such is Jesus himself; our reward comes from the mercy of God the Father.

If we are honest with ourselves, however (and how can a Christian afford not to be honest?), we must confess that doing good can be frustrating. Perhaps labeled, on the one hand, as a do-gooder, and on the other hand having much of our efforts to do good go unthanked and unrecognized or, perhaps, thwarted altogether, we might well wonder sometimes about the value of goodness in our fallen world. Surely the psalmist wondered as much: "Why do the wicked prosper?" Or, like Paul perhaps, we might sometimes wonder why we ourselves are capable of doing so little good. "I can will what is right, but I cannot do it. For I do not do the good I want, but the evil I do not want is what I do" (Rom. 7:18b-19). At times it indeed seems a struggle to do any good. How do we understand this?

In the context of Romans, Paul supplies an answer. It goes back finally to the absolute goodness of God. When God created this world, he created it according to his perfect, divine plan, and looking over each segment of his divinely ordered creation, "God saw that it was good." God can only create something good, because he is goodness itself. But humans have another capacity: to do good or evil.

We might imagine God's new creation as a tremendous work of art. Think of it as a perfect landscape painting done without flaw by the divine creator. The painting is complete, and it is good. And then man is put in the painting, and he has a bucket that is unopened. The bucket is filled with black, gooey tar. Man could have left the bucket closed. Instead, he opened that bucket and splashed wild, indelible globs of tar across the entire surface of God's painting. Nothing is left unstained or unaffected, so terrible was that action.

At a later day Jesus entered that painting and showed a way to clean up the mess. "Do good," he said, "even to your enemies." We know the painting will not be entirely cleansed until it is remade in the new heaven and new earth. It will take an act of God to redo the painting he created. Humans are much too puny to do it all, but we do have the help of a divine Savior in our effort. We are at work to redeem the earth with the help of Jesus, but to do so we must *do* good.

That, in a sense, lies behind Paul's thinking in Romans. Humanity also is stained with the tar and is incapable in itself of restoring the original. Paul gives another word regarding that tar: "It was sin, working death in me through what is good, in order that sin might be shown to be sin, and through the commandment might become sinful beyond measure" (Rom. 7:13). As long as we are in this life, our will to do good, and the good that we do, will be frustrated by sin.

But never does that imply that we should simply give in to sin. Redeemed people take a stand to bring redemption and to do good. Nurturing the fruit of goodness in today's world poses a challenge to the Christian, and one does well to bear these points in mind.

What is the source of goodness? Jesus himself said that "no one is good but God alone" (Mark 10:18b). God is absolute goodness, and he created a good world which humanity has marred. Because there is evil in this world, we are called to "hate evil, and love good, and establish justice in the gate" (Amos 5:15). Our encouragement to do good, then, comes from God who is goodness itself.

We remember, moreover, that our good deeds are in warfare against evil. We represent Christ on this earth and we also represent his warfare against evil. But how did Jesus engage in this warfare? By doing good deeds—healing the sick, providing for the improvident, restoring dignity and worth to the lost and pitiable. Here the lesson of Jesus takes on grave importance: "Then the righteous will answer him, 'Lord, when did we see thee hungry and feed thee, or thirsty and give thee drink? And when did we see thee a stranger and welcome thee, or naked and clothe thee? And when did we see thee sick or in prison and visit thee?' And the King will answer them, 'Truly, I say to you, as you did it to one of the least of these my brethren, you did it to me'" (Matt. 25:37-40). We do good in Jesus' name, and we do it to the least of these as he would have done.

Furthermore, we learn that we must not give up to the lure of complacence and be merely uncommitted do-gooders, working acts of kindness at our convenience. Paul writes frankly about his struggle with the flesh; but each of us has such a struggle. It is hard sometimes to motivate ourselves to do good. When our efforts flag, we would do well to think of Paul writing from his prison cell—or, better, to think of Jesus on the way to Calvary, when he said, "I made known to them thy name, and I will make it known, that the love with which thou hast loved me may be in them, and I in them" (John 17:26).

Finally, we remember that our strength in doing good is not our own but comes from the Almighty God whom we serve. On this faith, finally, our courage and conviction to do good rest. And our confidence also rests in the conviction that the Lamb of God will receive us at his throne and say, well done, good and faithful servant.

For Discussion

Why does the Christian do good works? Why don't we just ignore the world and concentrate on our eternal home?

Romans 2:6-7 says this about doing good works: "For he will render to every man according to his works: to those who by patience in well-doing seek for glory and honor and immortality, he will give eternal life." Paul speaks of an eternal reward for doing good works, but is there also a temporal reward? That is, what reward do you have now for doing good works?

What is the difference between being a do-gooder and doing good? We also have to ask this question: For whom do we do good works? In *Ordering Your Private World,* Gordon MacDonald writes that "We are naively inclined to believe that the most publicly active person is also the most privately spiritual. We assume the larger the church, the greater its heavenly blessing." How does such a perception throw out of balance the biblical view of doing good?

CHAPTER SEVENTEEN

GOODNESS
Unamazing Grace

We consider on the one hand the goodness we do for others, but on the other hand we place it in the perspective of the goodness God has done for us. That we call grace.

Grace is a great thing; we are accustomed to discovering it in great events. The miraculous healing of a son or daughter, the conversion of a sin-corroded life, the restoration of peace in a family ruptured by dissension: these are the yardsticks by which we often measure grace. Indeed, grace flows boundless and free, but often it is measured unexpectedly, in inches, during the course of a thousand little events in our daily lives.

Those inches accumulate into knowledge of Christ and his dealing with us. Like steps on a long walk, they are often individually forgotten. They ought not be; each step on the Christian's walk turns up epiphanies of grace—most often unrecognized until some particular milestone in that walk is reached. Sometimes, too, the walk may seem a darkness, a maze, a wandering. Perhaps at those moments abounding grace is most present and least detected.

But my concern here is with grace that springs up, untended and unexpected, in the humdrum little steps of life. Such grace is recollected in tranquility or anxiety, but often not until long after. Looking back is a good thing—not to try to redo the path but to know where we have walked and how we went there. Let me provide one example: the lesson of a battered camper.

We bought that camper for an unbelievably low price (we later discovered it was warranted and without warranty) in order to take a camping trip to California. This would enable me to keep my family with me during the long weeks of work that I would be putting in at Stanford University researching a book I was writing. It seemed an answer to our prayers. The prayers had scarce begun.

To begin, the trailer was a Wheel-Camper brand, made by a firm in Centreville, Michigan. Wheel-Camper went bankrupt during the gas crunch of the seventies. This camper of mine was an eleven-year-old model that suffered from at least ten years of bitter neglect. If parts were hard to get for more recent models, they were impossible to get for this one.

Not that I worried about parts at first. It was enough of a job to grease the wheel bearings. It took me four hours to do the first, only two to do the others. The problem was getting this ton of dead weight propped in the air while I wrestled tires in and out of a maze so tiny Houdini would have been amazed. How could all that weight balance on such small tubes? "Keep the air pressure up," the seller had told me. Fine. All I needed was a hovercraft.

Despite the grim omens, the trailer did well for over six thousand miles of our western excursion. It had the genuine feel of pioneering, covered wagon style. I checked the tire pressure with a faithfulness that I began to believe merited the grace I received of one more day of trouble-free driving. The days stretched into weeks, into a month, into Highway 80 in Nebraska on the Fourth of July.

Interstate 80 is a national disgrace among highways, a monument to the toll of travel in our nation. Ripped by behemoths on eighteen wheels or more, corroded by neglect, fractured by inept repairs at exorbitant prices, the road is a defiant challenge to the American wanderlust. Thirty miles west of Omaha some crew had ripped out four inches of pavement and, without advertising their efforts on a road sign, packed up for the holiday. When my camper hit the four-inch bump, it slewed suddenly like a wounded rhinoceros, tires clawing the pavement in billows of blue smoke. While traffic careened around me, I managed to wrestle the heaving load through another series of road gouges and off to the shoulder, near a sign which read UNEVEN PAVEMENT.

Uneven springs. One had broken gloriously, punching up

through the camper bottom where smoke and chewed asphalt gagged the contents. When a spring breaks, I learned, the wheels stop turning.

Being stranded thirty miles west of Omaha at 6 P.M. on the Fourth of July is no picnic, despite the fireworks that crackled in my mind. We left the camper stunned on the shoulder and set out on a search for a pay phone. The one we found had these instructions etched on a small metal plate above it:

STOP

1. Have 10 cents in Coins Ready
2. Listen for Dial Tone
3. Dial Number Desired
4. When Party Answers quickly Deposit coins

It was a juggling act, but a friendly one. When the serviceman I called answered, he reminded me as I fumbled for a dime, "I know you're there, buddy. Just put your dime in and you can talk to me. That's it. Now, what's the trouble?"

For the first time in over a month we slept in a motel while the camper went in for overnight service. We watched the holiday cascade of fireworks from Washington, D.C., on television. Later, we called it grace.

And I felt prepared should I ever break another camper spring. That was how I met Fred Rowan.

A year later we headed for a week to the great north woods of Michigan's upper peninsula, a region that has held a call to my spirit since my youth, a region of singular and unparalleled beauty. The gateway to it all is the spectacular, five-mile-long Mackinac Bridge. For me it is a psychological test each time I cross it. Suffering from acrophobia, I approach the bridge with hands white-knuckled on the steering wheel. A third of the way up its massive rise I'm fighting through to the eye of a hurricane of vertigo. People tell me the view at its peak is spectacular. Once I forced my eyes from locked-on-center to the side for a look. I saw water. Far, far below.

This time we approached the bridge towing the Wheel-

Camper in a blinding rainstorm with winds buffeting the length of car and camper. I hit the familiar rise to the bridge and felt the sickening lurch of the trailer as a spring snapped. There is no room to pull off on the Mackinac Bridge. Once on it, you're on for the duration. Cars don't break down on the Mackinac Bridge. Trailers don't break springs.

The rain I had been silently lamenting as my knuckles changed hue from tan to funereal gray was suddenly my ally. Call it grace if you wish. Without the slick surface, the wheel, trapped now on the axle, would have skidded and slewed. Instead, it dragged rigidly over the slick pavement as I kept the accelerator flat against the floorboard and dragged the ton of dead weight at 45 mph.

On the northern side we lurched off to the first available shoulder, a contemptible action that was getting all too familiar.

The phone booth, this one modernized and asking twenty-five cents per call, was a long walk away through chilling rain. A half dozen calls brought the knowledge that the closest trailer service center was at the Soo Locks, seventy miles north. But finally someone at one of the garages I called suggested that I try Fred Rowan.

"He'll fix ya most about anything," the man said. "Can't hurt none to try."

Certainly not. Not when one is out two dollars worth of quarters, soaked to the skin, and out of numbers to call anyway. Grace? Not abounding here.

The first thing that struck me when I called him was that this man had the sweetest, prettiest voice I have ever heard. Those are strange adjectives for a man's voice, but even over the phone the tenderness of that voice laved me like an absolution.

"Don't worry about it," he said as I tried to describe where my crippled beast lay wounded. "Wherever you are, I'll find you."

Who hasn't longed to hear those words? Wherever you are, I'll find you.

I expected, then, a saint to descend on my camper. But this was no Saturday-morning cartoon grace.

Fred Rowan ratcheted up in the most battered vehicle I've seen, a derelict from the fifties, a squat, ugly truck chewing up the dirt drive like an ulcerated tooth. Red letters barely discernible through the general decay of metal read FRED ROWAN MECHANIC ON WHEELS.

As I stepped out of the car to meet him, once again into the gusting rain, my wife called with wry cheer, "Ask him if he sells ice cream cones." Indeed, it looked like a badly used Good Humor truck.

Dressed in baggy soiled pants, a filthy coat already soaked with rain, and a cap too small and oddly angled on his head, Fred Rowan peered hard at the trailer. His hair was a close-cropped thatch of gray above a face so seamed and weathered it looked ancient, a dereliction of years and time's savagery embedded there like corrugations of grief. A cigaret smoldered perilously close to his lips.

But then again came that voice. "We'll fix you up in no time," he said, and the tones, the melody of that voice was—and I hesitate again at the adjective—angelic.

I wanted to believe him as he hauled grease-laden jacks and chains and bulky chunks of rock maple from his battered truck. He hunched and crawled in the muck for twenty minutes, got the camper squared away so that I could tow it following him to his garage five miles down Highway 2 at the pace of 30 mph. He set the pace. "I won't lose you," he said.

Fred Rowan figured it would take him about three hours to find a spring—he wasn't sure where, but he would find one—and install it. In the meantime, we got out of the rain by eating at a restaurant. In that way I received my final lesson in grace from Fred Rowan.

He was, I observed, a muscular, hard-working man under those tattered mechanics clothes, and a man who had worked with working men all his life. The first time I heard profanity in his sweet, gentle voice, I was startled. But that was part of my lesson. If Fred Rowan may have been unredeemed, for which I had little evidence one way or the other, he was still an instrument of grace. That is the hard lesson, one I mulled over as I sat with my family in the restaurant, watching gray rain slap against the windows and as I thought about Fred Rowan wrestling under my camper.

As veteran campers, my family knows when to use or not use a restaurant. On a long trip we have one meal a week in a restaurant—Sunday dinner, for example. Or we use them in dire emergencies, like the motel on our Fourth of July breakdown. Or the time we arrived in Needles, California, at 4 P.M. with the temperature at 115 degrees. I asked the campground owner which restaurants were air-conditioned in Needles. There were three: a McDonald's, a Jack-in-the-Box, and a Hobo Joe's. Hobo Joe's had an "eat all you can" fried chicken special. We ate all we could for nearly three hours in a temperature 30 degrees cooler than that outdoors. We left a very generous tip. I'll never forget Hobo Joe's, even though it was a long time before I could eat fried chicken again.

But this second thing about restaurants. I like to eat in small hometown restaurants, especially for breakfast. You get to know the people and the area fairly well during a leisurely hour in a corner booth. Who can forget walking into a restaurant in Orange City, Iowa, for the first time and receiving the "Sioux County Stare" as twenty heads swivel and rivet on the stranger walking in? The second time you enter they say hello. Who can forget the drugstore in Pennsylvania with a genuine 1950s soda fountain and hot fudge sundaes six inches high, around whose peaks one can observe a slice of America virtually unchanged for thirty years? It was the same in this restaurant in St. Ignace, Michigan, where we intended to eat away the better part of our wait. And each of my meetings brought me into a better understanding of Fred Rowan, working at his garage three miles away.

We were early, 4:30 or so, and the restaurant was quiet. But already one could spot the regulars. Over by the salad bar stood a white-haired man who looked like William Faulkner, a short man who walked slowly and with dignity, as if responsibility weighed on one shoulder and wisdom on the other. A busboy, a heavyset man in his twenties with thick lips and moon-shaped eyes, leaned over and swabbed our table with a rag. He grinned approvingly at us and moved on. "Is he handicapped, mommy?" asked our youngest. How does one begin to explain? Aren't we all?

The star of this small restaurant show was an elderly man dressed in clean but worn working clothes neatly pressed and snuggly fitted to his elderly but still firmly muscled body. He had a kindly, wrinkled face, like a Santa Claus in a July performance. He would take a sip of his coffee, then rise and walk to a table where children were seated. Magically a sucker appeared for this child, a Tootsie Roll for that. His fingers were quick, elusive, deft. They appeared from nowhere, these gifts. And in his high chanting voice, like a Robert Frost in the Midwest, he asked questions any child knows.

"And tell me, who's buried in Grant's tomb?"

"I don't know."

"Well, then, let me tell you a story of how Grant got there." And he gave a quick story, or a poem, having nothing to do with Grant. It was never the same story as he moved from table to table, his high, thin voice a bardic chant.

> Old bunny saw the October moon.
> Old bunny knew winter would be here soon.
> He climbed in his den,
> Said his prayers and then
> Bunny fell asleep in his bedroom.

And the children would giggle. Some rose and followed him. To older children he recited a longer ballad about a Lake Superior freighter that went down in an ice storm.

"Say," he exclaimed at one table, "do you know the largest freighter on the Lakes?" And he gave minute specifics of the ship—breadth, length, draft, tonnage. Or, at another table, "Did you cross the bridge? Yes? Did you know there are forty-two thousand miles of wire in the cables? Forty-two thousand! Do you know how high those towers are? Five hundred and fifty-two feet above the water!"

I grew dizzy. I had made it, once again, over this bridge. Delivered into the hands of Fred Rowan.

When we returned to his garage he was wrestling with springs, drills, and bolts under the camper.

"Well, how did you enjoy your dinner?" Again, that voice as

sweet as spring, soft and gentle. I didn't want him to hurry, although I was mindful of the fact that he had had no dinner yet. I wanted to stay and talk.

Did he know the man who told stories at the restaurant?

"Sure, I know Rufe Martin. Rufe Martin knows more about Michigan than most people, I'd say. He was a lumberjack until he retired. But he always read books. All kinds of books. He is a smart man, Rufe Martin. Lives in a rest home in Mackinaw City now, but every day he hitches a ride over the bridge with a work crew and walks the three miles to the restaurant. Three miles each way. Every day. There aren't many left like Rufe anymore."

"Why?" I asked. "Why the long walk each day?"

"This is his home. Here people listen to him. Isn't that what a home is for? Sure, I know Rufe Martin well. He's a friend from way back."

I found myself wanting to be friends with Fred Rowan. I realized that in another half hour or so I would probably never see this man again.

The door squealed open, admitting the rotund busboy from the restaurant. His wide lips split like fruit rind into a grin. "Hiya Fred!"

"Well, hello Bobby. How's my boy?"

My boy? Or my son? I don't know. But he talked to Bobby with the infinite grace and patience that marked everything he said or did, listening to questions of which I could decipher little meaning—"Fred, whaddya give a point fer a Ford?"

"Adjust the points, Bobby? Sure, I can do that. Let me finish this spring and we'll get your Ford running?" He said that like a question, as if honoring Bobby with the choice.

"Sure, Fred." They rattled on about the upcoming fair, about the weather. It was seven-thirty. The camper was fixed. We had a camping space reserved near the Soo Locks. I left with the spring repaired, glad to be on my way, a bit sad to be leaving.

It was a small lesson in grace, a moment slowed down in time's rapid turning, a moment that touches all successive hours and somehow makes them richer. Sometimes grace slips into our lives not like a lightning flash but like a small quiet light or like the soft sound of reassurance from a seamed and tattered man I'll likely never see again.

He was leaning against the doorway, chatting with Bobby as I pulled out of the driveway. He waved once, then walked through the rain toward Bobby's Ford.

For Discussion

Two items come to bear on unamazing grace. First, we discover how God's grace operates daily and consistently in our lives, often in ways we least expect. Second, we learn to appreciate the instruments of grace that God has blessed us with in this world. We may indeed entertain angels, although we remain unaware of that fact. Can you isolate instances of unamazing grace in your life? Perhaps they are not angelic but simply human— means of God's grace at work in our world.

Furthermore, you might identify a person who strikes you particularly as a means of grace. What qualities does that person's life exemplify?

CHAPTER EIGHTEEN

FAITHFULNESS
A Hero of Faith

In the third chapter of Galatians Paul refers to him as one of the great heroes of faith. The same designation occurs in Hebrews. And rightly so. He is one of the great heroes of faith.

Imagine Abraham in his homeland, a well-established man, comfortable and wealthy, "very rich in cattle, in silver, and in gold," and seventy-five years old. And then the call comes. We don't know just how, but the call was clear and specific—one of those startling intrusions upon a comfortable life when God reveals his plan. "Go from your country and your kindred and your father's house," says the Lord.

I, Lord? Where?

"To the land that I will show you."

Here is the first test of faith—not to such and such a named place where you will be guaranteed a raise in salary and a comfortable housing allowance. No, only to a place the Lord will show him. But, where? Don't ask, just go. Only these three things the Lord promises as comfort: (1) "I will make of you a great nation," (2) "I will bless you," (3) "and make your name great."

But, the human Abram might say, "I'm quite comfortable where I am. Thanks anyway." Might say, but doesn't. As an act of faith Abram does as he is told. He packs up and leaves.

And to what a land! Egypt in famine.

But this isn't the worst of it. To be sure, Abram is wealthy. But he is an aging man and he has obeyed an unusual order with an unusual promise—"I will make of you a great nation."

But when, Lord? Abram might say. Here's the problem. Sarah is barren. All these years. Abram says, "Behold, thou hast given me no offspring." Yes, we might sympathize with Abram in this trial by faith. How long he has awaited the promised offspring.

And the battles and struggles and trials that intervene! The trial when the herdsmen of Lot quarrel with those of Abram so that the two kinsmen separate, Lot choosing the fertile valley while Abram continues his wandering. The battle when Abram has to rescue his kinsmen from the hands of King Chedorlaomer. And the daily struggle to abide in God's will. And still the promise is reaffirmed: "Fear not, Abram, I am your shield; your reward shall be very great" (Gen. 15:1).

Like Abram, we cry out at different points in our life, "How long, Lord? You have all power! How long must we endure until your promises are fulfilled?" In the face of severe depression, when the afflicted Christian finds each new day an added darkness of unrelieved psychological suffering, we cry out, How long, Lord? In the face of unattenuated loneliness, when the single person looks at days and weeks and years of solitary life so that time itself becomes a threat, when that person feels she cannot face one more day alone, we cry out, How long, Lord? When we face the valley of sickness, when cancers corrode the body and the link to life seems so fragile, we cry out, How long, Lord?

Like Abram, who yearns for offspring, we cry out, How long, Lord?

And the word of the Lord comes: "I am the Lord." Trust me, Abram. My word is sure. Have faith in me. I will never forsake you. "I am the Lord." That is sufficient.

Here is the paradox, the tension of faith—giving up our worldly wants to the will of God so that our wants may be answered in his will. Let no one think faith is easy. There is a saying: "Let go and let God." How hard that letting go can be— but it is not until we let go the things we want, let them slide through our grasping fingers, that God will fill our hands to overflowing.

And here is Abram, ninety-nine years old, letting go. Too old, surely, to beget a child. But here's the miracle. It is not man's way that counts, but God's means. God's means always lie beyond the capability of humans. "I am God almighty," the Lord says to Abram. Don't you know this yet? There is nothing the Lord can't do. Indeed, Sarah shall beget a child. She shall be blessed. She laughs at this? At bearing a child at the age of ninety? Is there anything the Lord can't do? Here is a sign: The child shall be called *Isaac,* which means "he laughs." The Lord will have the final say here.

And this, too: your name shall be changed as a sign—from Abram, which means "exalted father," to Abraham, which means "father of many." Do you dare believe it?

It would seem the trial of faith is over when Isaac is born. The young lad Isaac grows in health. The promises have been affirmed. And then the terrible word, the word that strikes terror in Abraham's heart, comes to him: "Take your son, your only son Isaac, whom you love, and go to the land of Moriah, and offer him there as a burnt offering upon one of the mountains of which I shall tell you" (Gen. 22:2).

I must confess, I would have stayed home. I would have said, You can't mean this, Lord. I waited too long for that promise. And now this? You can't mean it. Sacrifice my only son? No, it is contrary to all the promises you have made. I see that clearly. You can't mean it. That is what I would have said—the coward's way out. I would see it this way.

But the Lord doesn't see as man sees. He sees down through all eternity, and he sees another sacrifice in the time of man.

Nor does Abraham see it that way; at least we have no record of such. The record is this: "So Abraham rose early in the morning, saddled his ass, and took two of his young men with him, and his son Isaac; and he cut the wood for the burnt offering, and arose and went to the place of which God had told him" (Gen. 22:3). Abraham knows the word of the Almighty Lord and is obedient to it.

Note this, however. Abraham knows from the outset, from the first step of his journey, that the end of his journey is to be the death of his only son. For three days he travels to Moriah with the terrible knowledge as the price of his obedience. What thoughts coursed through his mind? Did he think of a hundred years of yearning for this son? Did he think of the good times that boy had, of all that he promised as an adult—the seed of a great nation? We have no record. Only the lonely trip to Moriah, and on the third day, the arrival at the appointed place.

Abraham is an old man, too old to carry wood up the mountain. The wood is laid on the back of Isaac. His only son must bear the means of his own death. So they scale the mountain, until they arrive at the place where Abraham must arrange the wood and draw the knife. Isaac questions him: "Where is the lamb for a burnt offering?" And Abraham responds, "God will provide himself the lamb for a burnt offering, my son" (Gen. 22:7-8). Abraham arranges the altar, binds his only son to it.

Again, what thoughts must have coursed through his mind, for there is no human answer for this obedience. What might Abraham's people have said had they looked upon this lonely scene? Murder! they would have cried. Some would have said, This is mere foolishness. God can't mean this. It's stupid, Abraham! Still others, some of the pagans of the neighboring tribe, would have said, It's a sacrifice, of course. But it is none of these. It is a response in faithful obedience to the word of the Lord Almighty.

Of course we know the rest of the story. How the angel stopped the upraised knife by a command. How a ram was found caught in a thicket nearby and offered in Isaac's place. How Abraham called the name of that place "The Lord will provide."

Abraham's act of faith was carried down through the ages of biblical history with such resonance that the New Testament writers proclaim him a hero of faith. Abraham's faithfulness has lingered over Christian minds ever since. But above all, Abraham's act of faithfulness lingers over another lonely mountain, and another lonely sacrifice, when God led his son, his only son, in utter faithfulness to his promise of a redeemer for the world, to a sacrifice that could not be stopped.

In this sacrifice too there was loneliness and pain. God could have chosen not to do it. There is no one to dispute his word— except his own Word and his promise of one who would be bruised for our iniquities, wounded for our transgressions, one who would take upon himself the sins of the world. To his own word God is faithful and true. There is no human understanding for that act. It was terrifyingly lonely.

What thoughts coursed through the mind of God as his son, his only son, walked the hill of Golgotha? As Isaac bore the wood for the sacrifice on his back, Jesus bore his own cross on his back. Abraham may have thought of a hundred years of yearning for Isaac. God saw Golgotha looming on the dark horizon from all eternity. Abraham may have thought of the promised nation through Isaac's seed. God saw the nation of the redeemed led to eternal life through Jesus' blood.

Isaac questioned, "Where is the lamb?" Jesus prayed in the garden, "My Father, if it be possible, let this cup pass from me; nevertheless, not as I will, but as thou wilt" (Matt. 26:39). Was it possible for God to be unfaithful to his own word? To Isaac, Abraham said, "God will provide himself the lamb." God had declared Jesus, God himself, the Lamb, the one without blemish or spot, who would take away the sins of the world. Indeed, God did provide *himself*—his incarnate being—the sacrifice.

On Mount Moriah, at that terrible moment when Abraham raised the knife, God sent an angel to intervene. This was not to be the ultimate test of faithfulness. When he is seized for the sacrifice, Jesus says, "Do you think that I cannot appeal to my Father, and he will at once send me more than twelve legions of angels? But how then should the scriptures be fulfilled, that it must be so?" (Matt. 26:53-54). One angel stopped Abraham. A legion is a Roman military division of six thousand warriors. More than seventy-two thousand warrior angels stood at attention to come to Jesus' aid. To come *at once!* One angel destroyed Sodom! But the angels did not come—how then should the Scriptures be fulfilled? God's word is faithful and true. In place of Isaac a ram was found, but who else could stand in Jesus' place—stand as the son of God to fulfill God's word? Jesus is the offering, the perfect offering.

No, Abraham is not the absolute measure of faithfulness. Surely he is a hero of faith. But, finally, we look to Jesus, for here surely, on the dark mountain of Golgotha, God did provide. That is the place of our provision, the sacrifice and the place that makes our faithfulness possible and meaningful.

For Discussion

The short book of Ruth has one of the Bible's most moving stories of faithfulness in the midst of uncertainty and of faithfulness rewarded.

In the space of a decade Naomi's husband and two sons died, leaving Naomi, Ruth, and Orpah widows. When Naomi decided to go to Moab to find the Lord's favor, Ruth went with her. We remember Ruth's touching words of fidelity: "Where you go I will go, and where you lodge I will lodge; your people shall be my people, and your God my God; where you die I will die, and there will I be buried" (Ruth 1:16-17).

We are not told what would have happened to Ruth had she not gone—that is a story which didn't happen. Nor are we told what happened to Orpah, who did leave. We have only this tremendous testimony of the faithfulness of Ruth. But we do have the rest of her story, how she and Naomi were rewarded for their faithfulness.

Looking closely at the story of Ruth, we might well ask how her life demonstrates the fruit of faithfulness.

CHAPTER NINETEEN

FAITHFULNESS
The Great Risk; The Great Comfort

Rebuking his disciples for their lack of faith, Jesus said, "Truly, I say to you, if you have faith as a grain of mustard seed, you will say to this mountain, 'Move from here to there,' and it will move; and nothing will be impossible to you" (Matt. 17:20). A few days later, Jesus reminded them of this promise: "Truly, I say to you, if you have faith and never doubt, you will not only do what has been done to the fig tree, but even if you say to this mountain, 'Be taken up and cast into the sea,' it will be done. And whatever you ask in prayer, you will receive, if you have faith" (Matt. 21:21-22).

Can anything be clearer than that?

In a childhood game we played, a person had to do a complicated list of things before asking a question: twirl three times on one foot, say a complicated little tongue twister, hop five times, then ask a question. The question would be answered only if all the preliminary steps were successfully performed. Jesus' words, on the contrary, are so straightforward as to be simply astounding. Ask. Have faith.

This business of moving mountains is a curious thing. I can also recall, in my childhood, pondering that verse. It troubled me to no end. I envisioned mountains flying through the air, physically rising and moving like great UFOs from one place to another. And I wondered why my fly balls in our neighborhood baseball games failed to clear the home-run fence surrounding the playground. The verse seemed to offer so many delightful opportunities.

As a matter of fact, there is a literal, absolute truth to Jesus' statement. As creator of all heaven and earth, he literally has commanded the mountains to be moved and he really does have the authority and power to move them again any time that it pleases him. That time will come on the judgment day, when the earth will literally be shaken and be remade into the new heaven and earth. There is absolutely no question about the literal truth of Jesus' statement.

This absolute authority of the divine Maker appears often in the Bible in the image of the potter and the clay—but in this case God the potter not only shapes the clay but has in fact called the clay into existence. Therefore, the word of God comes through the prophet Isaiah, "Woe to him who strives with his Maker, an earthen vessel with the potter! Does the clay say to him who fashions it, 'What are you making'? or 'Your work has no handles'?" (Isa. 45:9). And Isaiah confesses in his own voice, "Yet, O Lord, thou art our Father; we are the clay, and thou art our potter; we are all the work of thy hand" (Isa. 64:8). In the New Testament Paul uses this same figure to affirm God's omnipotence: "Has the potter no right over the clay, to make out of the same lump one vessel for beauty and another for menial use?" (Rom. 9:21). According to Paul, God has made each of us according to his purpose and will, and our task is to be obedient to that purpose and will. Yes, literally and truly, God the Maker has the power and authority to move real mountains. In fact, in the act of creation he already has.

But that hard saying of Jesus may also be taken figuratively, for the mountains in our lives are not all physical. In the case of physical mountains, it is not for us to move *here* what God has planted *there*. Our faith is not to disrupt the order of God's creation. But there may very well be a figurative mountain in our lives that we by faith can ask God to move and it will be moved. By removing such a figurative mountain, God's order may be restored. What might such a mountain be? There are probably as many different mountains as there are individuals, for in this fallen world each person has some impediment, what Paul called his thorn in the flesh, that afflicts his fallen nature. For one person it may be the mountain of slavery to alcohol, a disorder in God's creation that can be removed by faith and prayer, as thousands of people in Alcoholics Anonymous can testify.

Now, two things about mountains and faith. First of all, we recognize that God's will is supreme, not our own. One of the most deadly errors we can make is to charge that if certain mountains are not immediately swept away in another person's life, then that person's faith must be lacking. The fact of the matter is that God may allow certain mountains to stand in our way in order to lead us *over* them, to make us stronger Christians because of our mountain climbing.

I will never forget a time early in my teaching career—at my first job, in fact. The house we moved to was at least eighty-five years old, a towering structure of brick with oak panels abundant both in the stairwell where the stained glass window admitted little light and in the receiving room, which, for lack of furniture, we kept closed off. The exterior brick was snugly fitted, having been repointed during the thirties, when quality masons were readily available. Moss covered the north and east sides where the damp cellar dove into the ground.

Below the sloping backyard, a cliff sprawled into the river that wound here through a tangle of shrubs and trees—many of them dead—before spilling over a dam where a grain mill once stood. All that remained of the mill were the white, protruding remnants of the foundation and the great grinding wheel, turned upright and embedded in the grass before the neighboring jail. Across the river on the opposite corner was an automobile agency, the owner of which stopped by the house to inquire about the status of my decrepit Chevy.

The Chevy was fine, thank you. But little else was.

It started our first night there. After a group of faculty members descended on the U-Haul and trundled boxes and crates to various rooms, after eating the brought-in meal of slightly cold lasagna, and after bedding down the two children, we didn't have the energy to put our bed together. We flopped the box spring and mattress down in the bedroom between piles of book boxes, arranged some hasty bedding, and fell asleep.

One should understand this: I was three years returned from Vietnam, a tour spent often in bunkers under exploding shells through two Tet offensives. My nerves were still not totally healed. I jumped at small, sudden sounds. I awakened often at night and paced the living room. I took long walks in the country, for hours, doing nothing but listening to small, expected sounds like the breeze humming or the birds singing. When an automobile passed by, I cowered inwardly and looked for a place to hide. Only my wife knew this—knew that it was necessary and that this too was healing. To all others I was simply a young scholar and recent recipient of a Ph.D. bound for his first full-time teaching position at a respectable, medium-sized private college in the east.

That, in part, explains the way it started I didn't know that atop the automobile agency was the fire siren for the local volunteer fire department. When it blasted at 2 A.M. that morning, my wife found me frantically trying to crawl under the box spring and mattress, finding no place to go since they lay on the floor. She comforted me, and we joked about it in the morning.

But there were other things that frayed at our nerves with hard, crooked teeth. Our son grew ill, and more ill; his fireball energy and relentless smile diminished to a wan grimace across pallid cheeks. We admitted him to the local hospital, which put him in a bed, shooed us out, and ignored him. We knew better, my wife and I, she especially with several years of nursing in major hospitals. But more, we knew the plaintive whimper of our son as we were ordered out of the hospital each evening at 8 P.M. After a week, and against medical orders, we simply lifted him out of the bed and left for home. And then our daughter, with her insatiable bent for investigating any oddity, wondered what it would be like to suck on the end of a clothes hanger and came tottering in her eleven-month-old fashion into the living room with the clothes hanger protruding through her lip, her clothes a growing puddle of blood. Those were some of the first steps she took, I remember now. That night she developed a cough and the ceiling above her bed was spattered with blood.

It was about then a stranger came by. She introduced herself by a name I didn't recognize, then stated directly: "Do you have any sins to confess?"

"No," I said, surprised. But found myself thinking, Good Lord, how many! And I have confessed them. "No," I said again.

"Yet you must," she insisted. "You're being persecuted for some secret sin in your life. You won't be free of this until you confess it."

My wife and I looked at each other, thanked her, and ushered her cordially out. Her meaning was clear—and vindictive. Because our faith was weak, she believed, we were finding mountains in our way.

But that wasn't the end.

There was the bat. That was, we thought, the last straw. It flew in through the fireplace chimney one evening as my wife and I dozed on the davenport, arms around each other in somnolent exhaustion. I seized a book and flung it. The bat wheeled, careened, and disappeared. But this, this creature, was still in my house. And the children were sleeping. I saw the creature at their necks.

I was not particularly afraid of bats. Throughout graduate school days I had gone fishing nearly every Saturday evening at any one of more than a dozen farm ponds within a five-mile radius of our house. I was friendly with the farmers. They knew me for my long walks in the country. They liked the way my son imitated the sounds of their cattle and fed them sweet clover with his small, fearless hand. I met the farmers at the church they had built with their own hands. And, after some careful but poorly disguised questioning on my part, they invited me to fish their farm ponds.

Nearly any Saturday evening around dusk would find me by one such, laying a hula popper expertly among some lily pads, probing the murky bottom with steady jerks of a purple "KilR Worm." And nearly any Saturday around 10 P.M. saw me heading home with Sunday dinner, four or five fat bass, in the yellow wash bucket. But in between dusk and 10 P.M. I shared the pond with a multitude of nocturnal creatures. The sonorous roar of bullfrogs careened among cattails, the thrash of a weasel on the distant shore, stray dogs yapping in the fields, and thousands of bats that swooped from the pine trees, arching and flicking at the tip of my fishing rod, dancing and flitting in the face of the rising moon. At the farm pond I was at home with them. But not in my home.

I called a friend I had made in those first days. He suggested placing raw hamburger by an open door. I did. A whole pound of it, strewn along the threshold and out the front porch. Follow that trail, I prayed. And I sat, the whole night, with a pot of coffee and a tennis racket, on the first landing of the stairs, also praying that I could kill it in one swift blow, a power smash maybe. Seldom have I prayed harder in my life than I prayed for vengeance that night.

The prayer wasn't answered. The days dragged by and the bat didn't appear. It's gone, we agreed. It found an opening and left. Bats can crawl through a hole the size of a pin head. Yes, it's gone. We didn't believe a word of it. Each morning my daughter complained of noises during the night, and we imagined the bat careening around her room.

It wasn't until two weeks later that the bat reappeared. I had been raking leaves outside and came to the table late. I still wore my old, indestructible Army boots, having paused only briefly to scrap the muck off against the concrete steps. We joined hands for prayer, each child in a high chair leaning across the trays with arms outstretched, my wife and I on the wooden chairs with the worn pads tied to their rails. The prayer ended with a piercing shriek from my daughter: "The bird is back!"

I echoed her shriek. For two weeks this had pent up in me. I ripped the foam pad from the chair, sending the chair hurtling across the room. In one vicious swoop I slammed the bat after it; as neat an overhand smash as I've done. The bat spun against the wall and slid down it to the floor. Its eyes glared at me with midnight hatred, its teeth bared in a primeval hiss of pure malice. Then the sole of the heavy Army boot ground it out. I got a roll of paper towels, cleaned the sodden mess up, ran outside and flung it far over the cliff and into the river. I watched until the ball of tissue disappeared over the dam.

When I returned my wife had the yellow wash bucket out and was crying and laughing at once while the children stared awestruck at their father's rage.

"It wasn't a bird," I said sternly to my daughter. "It was a bat."

"A bad bird," she said adamantly.

Those mountains weren't easy. It's never easy to see your children on the hospital bed. But God gave us a way over those mountains, and we—and our faith—are stronger for it.

But this second thing about mountains. Some of us, if we're honest, must confess that we rather like them. Like alcohol, some mountains are hard to give up. Giving them up entails some risk, a forsaking of a way of life that has become a comfortable pattern for us. That risk, I believe, is also suggested in the well-known definition of faith given in Hebrews 11:1, "Now faith is the assurance of things hoped for, the conviction of things not seen." There are two almost contrary parts to that definition—one of great surety, the other of great uncertainty. Study the words. *Assurance* and *conviction* speak to the great certainty. But of what? Things hoped for. Things not seen. What is so certain about that? We can't see, taste, touch, feel those things. They are abstractions—spiritual things, the things of faith.

We tend to place our assurance in less risky things. A home with a paid-up mortgage—there's assurance. Or a sizable pension plan, a solid IRA, perhaps a new car that we can be sure will start on winter mornings. And conviction? We are more likely to be convicted about tangible, planned, programmed things. But faith is not a computer.

In the Old Testament the Hebrew word for faith is used only twice; in the New Testament the Greek word for faith, as an active verb, occurs over 240 times. The word used for faith in the New Testament means, quite literally, to place yourself in Jesus. Faith and the Good News of the New Testament go hand in hand as one abandons old comforts and assurances and learns to walk hand in hand with Jesus.

Faith is the dynamic of Christian life—a way of walking through our life with complete and unshaken assurance that no matter what befalls us it will not make us fall out of touch with God. It is the steadfast belief that even if we don't always see the way clearly, Jesus has made a way for us and he will lead us on that way. Paul says that "we walk by faith, not by sight" (2 Cor. 5:7), and that in itself is an assurance, because we cannot always see the way ahead of us. Faith assures us that no matter what occurs, we too can lift the chorus "It is well, it is well with my soul." Even though we can't read every page in the book of our lives, we can sing that chorus because Jesus, who is "the pioneer and perfecter of our faith" (Heb. 12:2), has not only plotted the beginning, but he knows precisely where our earthly story will end.

Indeed, risk attends faith, but I prefer to reverse it. Instead of saying that we have assurance and conviction with risk, Christians can say that even though we have risk we have absolute assurance and conviction. Because Jesus was faithful, fulfilling the faithful prophecies on Calvary, even though the mountains may shake or rise up in our way, we have a faithful assurance.

And, finally, our assurance even among the great risks of life resides in the fact that God holds us along that way. In Isaiah 49:16 the Lord says "I have graven you on the palms of my hands." Do we understand that only as a metaphor, or as a life-shaping reality? Consider this. The Roman soldiers seized the carpenter Jesus and placed him against the wood of the cross. The carpenter learns to love the wood he works with, picking up the rich odor that escapes with each stroke of the adze, judging its grain immediately with a keen eye, assessing its strength or weakness. Except that this wood they laid Jesus against was the wood of the cross.

Then the soldiers picked up the carpenter's tools, the hammer and the nails. They didn't handle them carefully and lovingly: this was a work to be done quickly. They grasped the tools roughly, like novices, anxious to get on with the job. The nail was a jagged spike, meant to be driven in harshly to hold a joint tight. The spike was driven into Jesus' palms, where the hand meets the wrist, nailing the carpenter to the wood. His own tools turned on him. And thereby we, in the blows of the hammer on the spike, are *graven* on the palms of God's hands. Each blow of the hammer struck our name there: "For your sins he died."

Jesus, the carpenter. It is more than just a name, more than just a trade. Across the gulf of time and eternity Jesus the carpenter fashioned a bridge in the shape of a cross. Allowing himself to be nailed to it, he *became* the cross: the carpenter became the divinely crafted work and thereby gave us a way to be carried safely across that gulf, carried in his palms, in which our names are graven by the carpenter's nails.

Even when it seems we have to leap blindly by faith, he has prepared a place for us to land. To be sure, we will never find that place until we leap, but this promise endures: God has engraved our names on the palm of his hand, and it is his eternal hand that holds us when we leap out in faith.

For Discussion

In Romans 3:3-4 Paul asks, "What if some were unfaithful? Does their faithlessness nullify the faithfulness of God? By no means!" The significance of the passage is that God's faithfulness does not depend upon ours. What does this teach about God's sovereignty? How is it demonstrated in the Bible?

You might consider especially a passage such as Hosea 11. Are there examples in your own life of when God has been faithful to you, especially at a time when it was undeserved by any action on your part?

Søren Kierkegaard writes that faith is acted upon with "fear and trembling." Why is this so?

CHAPTER TWENTY

GENTLENESS
The Fruit of Courage

C. S. Lewis's Chronicles of Narnia have become, in the three decades since their publication, favorites of many children. Favorites of children and of a great many adults also. Perhaps those adults perceive things in the works that some children, some very young children, might miss. But all children who read these beloved adventures sense this much, I believe: the heroes and heroines of the works are all children themselves, but with special traits that endear them to the readers.

Those who achieve heroism in Narnia—Susan (who later falls from childhood belief), Lucy, Peter, Edmund, Eustace, Jill—are marked by no other trait quite so much as gentleness or meekness. Why this trait should be so attractive to today's children is a curious thing, especially since our children today receive the strong message from the secular world that only the strong survive. The popular media stars of our time strut across noisy stages full of glitter and pomp. There is not an iota of gentleness about them. This is the world's message: success (and that is the world's goal) derives from *power*, and it carries in its train wealth, fame, and glory. But Lewis offers a strange kind of glory: the glory of Christian gentleness. There are some very good reasons why Lewis does this.

In each of the stories the children are pitted against precisely the kind of proud power our world glorifies. They cannot defeat this power in their own strength, but only through faith in the great lion, Aslan. One of the children is himself a bully before being transformed by the lion. Eustace Scrubb enters Narnia as—there is no other way to put it—a brat and a bully. He lusts after power and is as greedy for wealth as the dragon of ancient mythology. One shouldn't be surprised, then, that he changes into a dragon and that he can't be freed to be *himself* until he submits to the claws of the lion to rip the dragon skin off from him. Only Aslan can transform him. In their own ways, each of the children is transformed by Aslan, transformed to loyalty and gentleness in the name of a supreme, divine king.

Behind Lewis's deceptively simple stories for children lies the author's brilliant academic career in medieval literature. It is in part from medieval tales that Lewis borrows one pattern for gentleness. Gentleness was one of the most cherished and honored traits of the medieval knight, who would swear allegiance to his sovereign king, and in the name of that king work in gentleness to bring justice to the world. Often he fought against the "bullies" of his age. But—and here is the significance—only the bravest and noblest of the knights were worthy of this calling to gentleness. In Lewis's conception, gentleness is *never* a mark of weakness; rather, it is the mark of the strongest and bravest.

As a Christian author, however, Lewis had another pattern for gentleness, sometimes called "meekness" in the Bible. Christianity also holds that the strongest are those who dare to be gentle. There are good reasons for this. First of all, if the Christian is to witness to the world, he won't get very far with arrogance and aloofness. The Christian life is a ministering life, drawing on a gentleness that demands strength and endurance. It is not surprising that Paul writes that "the Lord's servant must not be quarrelsome but kindly to every one" (2 Tim. 2:24). Some versions of the Bible have "gentle" rather than "kindly" in that passage. In his letter to Titus, Paul also encourages us "to speak evil of no one, to avoid quarreling, to be gentle, and to show perfect courtesy ["meekness" in some versions] toward all men" (Titus 3:2). The reason for this is clear, as James points out: our strength comes not from this world but from above, and "the wisdom from above is first pure, then peaceable, gentle, open to reason, full of mercy and good fruits" (James 3:17). Clearly, these ideals, which were so cherished by the medieval knights and which are modeled by Lewis's children in the Chronicles of Narnia, find their origin in Scripture.

But there is a second motivating factor for Christian gentleness. The secular world today earnestly believes that power and strength are the same thing. If one assembles enough of the symbols of power—prestige, money, fame—that person is strong and need not be gentle. As the book of Proverbs amply testifies, this is a foolish mistake. Indeed, the way of the world is foolishness. The mistake lies in equating strength with possessions, which all too quickly wither and pass away. Strength comes from authority, from giving and not from taking or accumulating. In the Christian life the source of strength is the almighty and absolute authority of God omnipotent. David clearly recognized this: "Thou hast given me the shield of thy salvation, and thy right hand supported me, and thy help made me great" (Ps. 18:35). This is a beautiful testimony to the absolute source of strength in God. Nowhere does David credit himself; God is the protector, God the right hand of support, God has made him great. Herein lies the Christian's source of strength, and his power to do acts of gentleness.

One might be surprised at the people of the Bible who are described as gentle or who bear this fruit. One would not immediately consider Moses a meek or gentle man. He grew up in the court of Pharaoh. He was exiled when his hot temper led him to murder. After being appointed by God to lead the people out of bondage, his temper again got him into trouble on several occasions, most notably when he grew impatient with God and struck the rock, a rash act for which he was not permitted to enter the promised land. But how does the Word of God describe Moses? Like this: "Now the man Moses was very meek, more than all men that were on the face of the earth" (Num. 12:3). Wherein did Moses' meekness lie? Is this a well-kept secret? Actually we find it revealed on numerous occasions.

Moses was God's appointed, and he did rely on God's strength. In fact, Moses protests that in himself he can do nothing—he is not articulate, not a forceful speaker, and he doesn't trust his own temper. But he does rely on God's strength and leading. Second, we observe Moses' meekness in his frequent intercession for the people of Israel before God. Time and time again Moses went before God to beg forgiveness for the sins of Israel. He loved the people and exercised gentleness to them. Third, we see Moses' meekness in his faithfulness. A lesser man might well have thrown up his arms in despair many times during those years of desert wandering, but Moses remained faithful to the task to which God appointed him. Perhaps Moses would not make it as a superstar, but he was a biblical hero, serving the Lord in gentleness and faithfulness, relying on God's power and acting in love toward the children of God.

We see, then, that it takes strength and courage to be gentle and that the source of the Christian's strength lies in God. But what is the Christian's *motivation* to gentleness? Why bother with *this* fruit? Yes, one can clearly see the importance of faith, of love, of joy and peace. But gentleness? Why should one bother with that?

We would do well to ask that question of Jesus, for he is the answer. Paul writes, "I, Paul, myself entreat you, by the meekness and gentleness of Christ" (2 Cor. 10:1). Paul entreats the Corinthians here not only by the power and authority of Jesus but also by his model of gentleness and meekness. The fact of the matter is that the Lion of Judah, the almighty and absolute Ruler, the King of kings came into human life as the Lamb of God who was gentle and meek and thereby bore our sins and infirmities. No, Jesus didn't have to be gentle. But he was strong enough to be gentleness itself, to submit to death for our everlasting life.

Here, then, is the glory of gentleness. In it we obtain our strength, our rich fruit, for in it we are acting as Jesus in this world. It is true that the world is not going to reward us with fame, power, and prestige for our gentleness. It certainly didn't reward Jesus. But there is a more glorious expectation that awaits the Christian than worldly praise: the promise of being received at his banquet table at the royal feast for the redeemed children of God. There is little we can bring to that table, but if we bring the fruit of gentleness we will be making a rich offering to the feast.

The tragedy is that so many people will choose not to come to that feast.

When we lived on a farm, I grew especially attached to both the wild, rugged countryside and to the birds and animals of the region—especially the birds, which were so prolific in the nearby forests and fields. Red-winged blackbirds nested in the meadow; cardinals flocked in the trees; hummingbirds, chickadees, hawks, and even owls seemed to be everywhere. I remember especially the spring that we found a baby robin that had fallen from its nest and how we nursed that little bird to health, in time letting it fly free from the nest of our family. We sometimes imagined that the robin returned to sing in the hickory in the backyard.

Knowing my love for birds, knowing that I missed them when we moved to the city, my wife gave me a finch feeder and five pounds of thistle seed for a birthday present a few years ago. I set it out that afternoon and watched by the window. No birds came; not that day or for days thereafter. To encourage the finches I built other feeders for other species and placed them about the yard. I hung suet. I put out pounds of good feed.

As I watched the untouched feeders I felt a touch of despair. Here I threw a party—no, a banquet—and nobody came. What an insult. And standing there by the window I began to understand Jesus' parable of the wedding feast. Yes, I would take birds from the byways, any that wanted to come and eat of the banquet I had prepared.

In time the birds came, of course—finches, cardinals, sparrows by the score, wrens, and others. They just had to find their way to my feeders, and it took a little time. But that other lesson remains. Jesus stands with open arms at his banqueting table, filled with the food of everlasting life. He stands waiting . . . waiting.

And we? Do we stand waiting? Or do we come with the fruit of gentleness, an offering to the strength and authority he has given us?

For Discussion

Each of us can probably name one event in the last week where we failed to maintain gentleness. We believed we were right and were determined to make that "rightness" known. It is easy to think about acting in gentleness; it is much harder to maintain it in daily living.

One help in maintaining the spirit of gentleness is to maintain a sense of goal. Jesus said, "Blessed are the meek." And how shall they be blessed? "They shall inherit the earth." Sometimes we believe, like the prodigal son, that we want our inheritance now, and we force our point of view upon others to get our "rights." The key lies in this fact: Jesus has an inheritance for the meek. He will bless them. The task until that time is to maintain gentleness.

A good way to get at this is to ask what kinds of behavior are opposed to gentleness? How might we have handled a situation during the last week in gentleness? Can we plan ahead for possible gentle responses to tense situations?

CHAPTER TWENTY-ONE

SELF-CONTROL
Warning Flag or Green Light?

Self-control! The word rises like a red warning flag before us in times of crisis.

The business executive has had a brutal day. It began before dawn—a few quick calisthenics, a too-short time for devotions, a breakfast gulped and washed down with a sea of black coffee. Then early to the office, flicking on the fluorescent lights that glare against voiceless machinery—typewriters, computers, copy machines. The day begins in a rip and unravels from there. The handouts for the meeting are late. The notes misfiled. By noon ragged sheets of lightning buzz in the executive's brain. Self-control!

The mother bundles her three children off for the school bus only to discover a lunch pail left behind. She races down to the corner only to catch the exhaust smoke of the bus in her face. Self-control!

The word has a sense of desperation about it—unraveling lives, harried thoughts, cross words, a last-ditch effort to salvage something positive out of a day.

And, then too, self-control sometimes suggests a lifelong effort against a wrong. Self-control always seems to arise in conflict—our sense of doing something wrong that we know full well we shouldn't do but can hardly help doing. Self-control arises at the ragged ends of life, almost always in a desperate effort to hold the ends together.

Sound familiar? It should. I don't know of a single Christian serious about his or her Christianity who has not struggled with self-control. But self-control can be more than a momentary effort to battle against the loose ends. Let me give one example—my own.

I have been in what now seems to have been a nearly lifelong battle against smoking. I smoke a pipe. I smoke it a lot and have done so since I was a teenager. I love to smoke. It relaxes me. It makes me feel good. And maybe a pipe isn't really so harmful after all. Those are the things I keep telling myself—and I know they're wrong.

So wrong, in fact, that I am also a confirmed quitter. Then I tell myself other things. Pipes stink. Smoking yellows your teeth, wrinkles your skin. Any smoking—pipe, cigar, cigaret—contributes to cancer, heart disease, a dozen other ailments. Those are the other things I keep telling myself, and I know they're right.

The conflict is one of self-control.

Now, I have quit smoking so many times I have lost count. The longest I have gone without smoking is seven months. I put on twenty pounds in the first month. That isn't so bad, I was told. Extra weight isn't as serious a health risk as smoking.

Right, I agreed, as I waddled to the refrigerator.

That time lasted nearly seven months and well over twenty pounds. And how did it end? As simply as this. I still went every day to the corner store in order to pick up a newspaper. I lived in a small Pennsylvania town then, and there was no home delivery of the paper. Besides, the walk to the store took off pounds. I used to buy my tobacco there, too, but I now reached for a candy bar instead.

Then one day I missed. That's right—it was all a matter of bad aim. (Do I need to remind you that the Hebrew word for sin literally means "missing the mark"?) Instead of a candy bar, there was a can of tobacco in my hand, much to my surprise. Since it was there anyway, I paid for it. Now the problems started.

I walked home wondering what to do with that can of tobacco in my pocket. Well, why not try a puff and see what it tastes like. Let's remember what we have put behind us—that is, behind a me large enough by now to be an "us." But I couldn't stoke up in front of the family. Where then? Oh, of course, in the sunny, secluded nook behind the garage! And there I sat like a little boy merrily puffing away.

And that wasn't the worst time! One night, under moonlight, I buried all my tobacco in the compost heap. The next noon I was scrounging for a little dry flake.

This is a serious problem in self-control. And believe me, I have tried *every* technique. I have a medical journal with full-color pictures of diseased organs! I have a drawer crammed with motivational literature, stop-smoking pills, nicotine chewing gum, and other things.

I take small comfort in the story of a well-known evangelist who was hooked on cigarets. One evening he soaked his cigarets in water and dumped them in the garbage. The next morning he was drying the cigarets in a toaster to smoke them.

It's laughable; it's sad. Is it beyond my control? I'll keep fighting until I find out. I would like to tell a happy story here of how I was able to give it all up and praise the Lord. But I can't tell that story. Yet.

The sad fact of fallen nature is that self-control is a ceaseless battle, and we are not always victors. Perhaps we can't defeat the problem entirely, but we can fight to control it.

This one thing is certain: if I had not started, I wouldn't have this trouble stopping. The best sort of self-control is the sort that occurs before the event. *Prepare* is a very important verb in the Bible—active and forceful.

King David had a problem that called for self-control. After years of preparation in the desert, God established him as king over Israel. He was a great king, a king of God's choosing and after God's heart. The kingdom was marvelously blessed under this ideal ruler who "administered justice and equity to all his people" (2 Sam. 8:15). One reason for its success, beside the obvious fact of God's blessing, was that David ruled justly and equitably, looking not to himself first, but to his people. In short, David exercised self-control. He put others before himself.

But then a sad thing happened in the peaceable kingdom. David grew too much at peace. He let his own personal defenses down. We read in the second book of Samuel that "In the spring of the year, the time when kings go forth to battle, David sent Joab. . . ." It was the time when kings went to war, but David was at ease. He sent his general, while he stayed home. David did what he could, not what he should.

At his ease in Jerusalem, relaxed on his couch, David wandered across his rooftop. He was bored. He was an accident waiting to happen. His guard was down and he was ill-prepared for what he saw—Bathsheba, the beautiful wife of Uriah, who was out fighting his war for him. We know the rest of the story. David lost control and initiated a chain of events that led to Uriah's death, his marriage to Bathsheba, the terrible warning of Nathan the prophet, and the death of the child that Bathsheba bore.

The lesson is terrible but simple. Yes, David lost self-control, but well before that he had failed to prepare himself. He did what he could, not what he should, and as such he was easy prey for temptation.

Two crucial messages about self-control emerge here, and they bear profound spiritual importance for us today. First of all, self-control begins in careful preventive maintenance, in careful preparation to avoid situations where control might be lost. I know a counselor who recognized in his own life precisely the sort of temptation David faced. It worried him considerably, but he took active steps to prevent it. First of all, he put a window in the door of the office where he counseled, and although the glass was frosted, it served as a link to the outside world. Second, he placed large photographs of all his family members, especially of his wife and children, around the office. He framed his children's drawings and hung them on the walls. He prepared carefully so that he wouldn't be placed in a situation where he might lose control.

The plain facts are that such situations do arise in this fallen world, that Satan will use whatever snares and deceits he can find to get his hook in the Christian's heart, and that the Christian had better do some preparation in self-control to meet those snares. In his letter to the Corinthians, Paul likens this preparation to that of an athlete getting ready for a race. It would be one foolish and embarrassed athlete who tried to compete in a marathon without weeks of prior training and warm-up exercises before the race itself. Paul concludes that "every athlete exercises self-control in all things. They do it to receive a perishable wreath, but we an imperishable" (1 Cor. 9:25). Our preparation ought to be all the more severe, Paul suggests, because the spiritual competition in which we are engaging is *the* big event of our lives and all eternity. No one wants to stumble or drop out of that race.

Paul is often fond of athletic imagery in his letters. I would hazard a guess that he was a man who loved athletic competition—and who had substantial physical endurance himself. In that regard he makes an interesting analogy in the next two verses, noting that "I do not run aimlessly, I do not box as one beating the air; but I pommel my body and subdue it, lest after preaching to others I myself should be disqualified" (1 Cor. 9:26-27). We must strive for self-control with all the earnestness and persistence that an athlete exhibits in training for competition. In Paul's terms, we might have to "pommel" ourselves to prepare.

Preparation, or preventive maintenance, is one key component of self-control, then. In this we look ahead. Knowing that we will be tempted, we prepare beforehand to meet the temptation. It may be a very simple thing. Coming home after a harried day at work, we might deliberately compose ourselves before entering the house to be with our family. This is a step I have to go through often. After a busy day at work, which often strains my own self-control, I have to deliberately tell myself to set it aside. Look, I say to myself, you're going home to the most precious treasure God has given you on this earth. In fact, it is the one treasure, and the only one, that you can take to heaven with you. Somehow, preparation in that perspective changes things.

If the first step in self-control is to take preventive measures, the second step is to learn to say no. Solomon wrote that "a man without self-control is like a city broken into and left without walls" (Prov. 25:28). The word *No* forms the armament and protective walls of the spiritual city. The story of Joseph parallels that of David, though with different action and different result.

This time Joseph himself was the object of the wanton glance, for he was, we are told, "handsome and good-looking" (Gen. 39:6). Joseph's master in Egypt, a man named Potiphar, had a wife who looked once too often on this handsome man and forthrightly invited him to lie with her. What was Joseph's response? He not only said no but he literally ran from that place with the woman tearing at his clothes. He was cast into prison as a result, but that was a small price to pay, for we read that "the Lord was with him; and whatever he did, the Lord made it prosper" (Gen. 39:23).

Sometimes *No* can be a hard word to say, but it is the key to self-control, the word that the Lord blesses.

A yet more compelling example of self-control comes from our Savior himself. One thinks of that lonely garden in Gethsemane where Jesus prayed to his father in an anguish beyond belief. Here the Son of God knelt and prayed "Not my will but thine be done." We must remember that Jesus could have called those legions of angels, that he had power and authority. And yet with that power only a prayer away, he subjected himself to the brutal torture, mockery, and death on Calvary so that those he loves and those who love him may be free. Jesus exercised self-control to free us.

Therein lies our pattern for self-control: to put others before ourselves and to put Jesus before all others. It is true that all our efforts at self-control will not be entirely successful. We still fight the "old man" in us and Satan outside of us. But a large part of self-control is persistence in the battle, continuing steadfastly to claim that because we are free in Jesus, we are free indeed.

The fruit of the spirit, we have seen, are rooted in the True Vine which is Jesus, and love seems to be the central, supporting vine. In a very real sense, however, self-control may be one of the chief and most necessary activities in relation to all the spiritual fruit. For example, only by careful self-control can one exercise the necessary pruning of the spiritual fruit, uprooting weeds, separating counterfeit fruits. And the counterfeit fruit of self-control may well be the self-righteousness that believes everything is in order, that the spiritual garden is just fine, thank you, and needs no further discipline. But in another sense, self-control is the full fruition of the spirit. Peter makes the point quite clearly: "Make every effort to supplement your faith with virtue, and virtue with knowledge, and knowledge with self-control. . . . For if these things are yours and abound, they keep you from being ineffective or unfruitful in the knowledge of our Lord Jesus Christ" (2 Pet. 1:5-6a, 8).

For Discussion

Self-control seems to be sufficiently clear. We have to exercise control over those areas of our self that are not pleasing to God. But is that the whole of the story when one considers the fruit of the spirit?

The difficulty with a negative approach to a fruit such as self-control is that it focuses backward on the problems we have had in the past and our need to exercise control over those problem areas. To be sure, we do well to learn from the past, but self control involves more than merely pruning weeds, however important that may be. Rather, like all the fruits of the spirit, self-control should be understood first as a way of living that is pleasing to God. In that sense, we might consider self-control a bridle and reins by which we steer our course, purposefully and with direction, in the way of God. And God's hands are also upon those reins.

The key to understanding the fruits of the spirit is realizing that each of them, self-control included, is a dynamic, active way of Christian living. The question here is how to understand self-control positively, looking ahead to the way God has provided.